Michèle Roberts is the author [illegible] *A Piece of the Night* (1978), *The Visitation* (1983), *The Wild Girl* (1984), *The Book of Mrs Noah* (1987), *In the Red Kitchen* (1990), *Daughters of the House* (1992) which won the WH Smith Literary Award and was shortlisted for the Booker Prize, *Flesh & Blood* (1994) and her most recent, *Impossible Saints* (1997). She has also published short stories, *During Mother's Absence* (1993), and three collections of poetry, including *All the Selves I Was: New and Selected Poetry* (1995). An occasional presenter for BBC Radio 3's 'Nightwaves', she is also a regular book reviewer.

Half-English and half-French, Michèle Roberts lives in London and Mayenne, France.

Titles by Michèle Roberts

FICTION

A Piece of the Night
The Visitation
The Wild Girl
The Book of Mrs Noah
In the Red Kitchen
Daughters of the House
During Mother's Absence
Flesh and Blood
Impossible Saints

POETRY

The Mirror of Mother
Psyche and the Hurricane
All the Selves I Was

Michèle Roberts

FOOD, SEX & GOD

ON INSPIRATION AND WRITING

A *Virago* book

Published by Virago Press 1998

A CIP catalogue record for this book is available from the British Library

ISBN 1 86049 455 2

Typeset in Garamond by M Rules
Printed and bound in Great Britain by
Clays Ltd, St Ives plc

Virago
A Division of
Little, Brown and Company (UK)
Brettenham House
Lancaster Place
London WC2E 7EN

CONTENTS

3 On Certain Writers

CONTENTS

6 On Writing

INTRODUCTION

Sometimes, when people I've just met discover that I write for a living, they ask me what I write about. I never know what to say. The title of this book refers to the answer I shall give next time I'm asked. It's as helpful, or as unhelpful, as any other.

Over the years I've written bits and pieces of non-fiction, some of which are collected here. Since they are all commissioned pieces they vary in tone, according to where they ended up. Taken out of context they can sound a bit odd, but I decided not to rewrite them but to let them stand as they are. I've divided them into six sections, according to theme. Some of the earlier pieces make me smile a bit now. Some of the ideas and thoughts I would express now in a different way or disagree with. They are all various shots at sorting out obsessions around writing and language and sex. I haven't done with them yet, thank goodness, and in this book I've changed my mind about them quite a few times, as you'll see, if you read on. I hope you enjoy the book and find something in it that speaks to you, a conversation we can share. That the book is published at all is due to my editor Lennie Goodings, and I'm very grateful to her for suggesting its compilation. I'm also grateful to Sarah White, who saw the book through the production process.

My deep thanks go to all the people, too many to name, whose ideas have helped to shape mine. Without them these essays could not have been written. One of my muses is my mother. This book is dedicated to Monique Roberts, with love and thanks for all she has given me.

Michèle Roberts, London, 1998

1

On Imagination

THE PLACE OF IMAGINATION

The Cardiff lecture, 1994

My thoughts about writing have developed as a result of *doing* it, of wrestling with the endlessly fascinating problems it poses as a *practice*, then trying to solve these through the process of creating forms that embody and express them. Writing contains talking-to-oneself-about-writing.

Conversations with other people about it can also be stimulating. From time to time I teach creative writing courses, and I find that the students' questions keep me on my toes and push me to search for answers, or at least for suggestions about possible routes to take. You learn a great deal this way, when students prod for your views on whether a piece of writing works or not and *why*.

Conversations with people in the audience at readings can be similarly productive. Our busy modern lives allow us little time for sitting around telling each other about what we like reading. This is a shame, since the company of passionate readers is so invigorating. Here tonight I feel I'm in the company of passionate readers and writers; it's a privilege and a delight to have the chance of discussing writing with you.

One of the questions I'm most frequently asked at public readings is whether my writing is autobiographical?

It sounds innocuous enough. But I've begun to wonder why,

every time this question is asked, it bothers me so much, to the extent that I become unusually bland and polite in answering it, a sure sign that I am harbouring repressed feelings of some sort.

The questioner might have all kinds of reasons for asking whether my work is autobiographical. He or she might have learned in school or in a writing class: write about what you know; and might want to find out what I think about the injunction, what it actually means. He or she might be asking the question simply to be polite and kind and find *something* to ask this writer who has invited questions and who is looking so in need of conversation. He or she might have heard the question asked at other readings and have concluded it's a question that you must always ask.

Both men and women ask me this question, but a quick poll of the writers among my acquaintance tells me that it is mainly the women who are asked if our writing is autobiographical. As though this kind of writing comes more naturally and easily to women, for some unspecified reason, and so is to be expected from us.

I'm uncomfortable with this question partly because it's posed in such either/or fashion, seeming to require a simple 'yes' or 'no' in reply, whereas I can't answer it like that. And it feels vaguely accusatory, this question, as though I'm being somehow policed, checked up on, rated. The answers it appears to solicit tumble out defensively. Either: no of course not, don't be silly, I am a Real Writer who uses my imagination; or: er, yes, deeply so, I'm afraid, but I'm not ashamed of it either.

It's *my* problem, isn't it, this paranoid feeling of being attacked and criticised, this sense of needing to justify and explain, rather aggressively mutter my doubts. Nonetheless, it forms part of the subject of tonight's lecture. I'm going to explore this problem and see where it takes me, in this time we've got together, and of course I hope that you'll accompany me, even though some of you may be wondering here at the outset: is this journey really necessary?

I shall speak personally, with no assumption of detachment or objectivity, since the subject arises in my own experience as a writer and it would be foolish to pretend otherwise. But I hope it may touch on your own interests and perhaps enter into dialogue with them. All of you, I am sure, are readers. Many of you, I am equally certain, are also writers, and may also have encountered this difficulty. I'm going to use this problem of autobiography – whether or not I can say my work is autobiographical – in order to explore one or two aspects of how the imagination works in writing and in daily life. I hope you will feel that what I shall say touches on your own concerns as people absorbed with the need to live and work creatively.

So what's my discomfort about? Why should anyone care very much whether or not the fiction a novelist writes is autobiographical? I'm afraid that I suspect my questioner in the audience of being less than innocent, of seeking to pigeonhole and control me by asking that blessed question. Autobiographical writer. Tick. Good, got that one labelled. As one might say: black writer, Welsh writer, feminist writer. Tick. Good, got *that* one pigeonholed. As though to suggest: partial, provincial, not really sophisticated. Perhaps I also suspect my questioner in the audience of seeking to satisfy his or her curiosity: did I really murder my aunt/make love to four men at once/give birth to triplets/travel by bicycle to Tibet? Whereas I want to tease and titillate and not tell you what's a lie and what's the truth. Oh you storyteller, as my grandmother used to say disapprovingly. Worst of all, I suspect my questioner of equating writing autobiographically with writing fiction that lacks art, lacks imagination. So that if I'm seen to write autobiographically then I'm automatically seen to possess inferior capacities as a writer.

Is this last a view being imposed on me from outside, as it were, or do I, deep down, secretly agree with it? If my own view of writing autobiographically is really so negative, then no wonder I want to deny doing it.

Shutting off a problem, denying its existence, of course never helps in the long run. Since writing fiction is, on one level, all about posing oneself literary problems of form and then trying to solve them by writing novels or short stories and discovering just what one can do with the form, playing with it, reinventing it each time, it strikes me that it might be useful to look at the question in terms of narrative perspective.

Whose narrative opposes imaginative and autobiographical writing? Who's telling the story about writing that sets up a standard against which I measure myself or might be measured? Whose words define success, award approval? Whose story *is* this?

Listening hard, I distinguish two quarrelling voices, each one representing a particular, apparently commonsensical view.

If I reply to my questioner: no, I don't write autobiographically, then I'm speaking with the voice of my education, convent grammar school in London followed by a degree in English Literature at Oxford, an education that in those days, back in the fifties and sixties, seemed to express eternal and transcendent truths, at least to my naive adolescent mind. This voice that I can hear speaks – and of course here I'm simplifying enormously – from a tradition which makes rigid separations between things regarded as different: thought and feeling, reasoned argument and emotional response, our inner lives and the outside world, sanity and madness, truth and falsehood. In this tradition a strong division is made between the artist's self and the work he or she produces, and certainly between the artist's body and the work produced. The body doesn't matter; it's the work that's significant, that will endure, its autonomy confirming its beauty, which we can then invest with all our longings for perfection and immortality. In the visual arts, the long and distinguished tradition of self-portraiture might be held to have successfully broken through this separation of artist and work. I'd argue, however, that the self-portrait, however apparently naked and raw, can still be seen, if the viewer so chooses, as a work of art that negates the body that produced it. And even though cultural theorists, again mainly but not only in the field of the visual arts, have begun to discuss The Body exhaustively, it's often in terms that keep it safely abstract, *dis*-embodied. The taboo still operates. You can see its power when it's breached in direct ways. Here I'm thinking of the upset provoked by Mary Kelly's seventies piece, *Post Partum Document*, which juxtaposed babies' nappies with bits of heavily theoretical text, thereby breaking through two barriers at once, linking art to text and linking body product to art product. Or, more recently, for example, there is work such as that by Damien Hurst which makes the bodies of dead animals part of the work of art. Other artists employ human blood, hair and body tissue. Part of the upset greeting such work, and the anger it can cause in the spectator, comes, I think, from the feeling: these things are *in the wrong place*; stained nappies are all very well soaking in a bucket or disposed of in a bin but have no place whatsoever in something calling itself art; similarly, parts of the human body must be kept rigidly separate from oil paint and canvas. Or else some sort of chaos will ensue. I'll explore later on what sort of chaos that might be. Here I just want to note that the taboo still operates for writers too.

In the medium of language, in the work of writing fiction, certainly in that sort of fiction which aspires to being called literary (*as opposed to* all the other sorts) we have retained a dominant notion of the writer striving to imitate a transcendent God creating something out of nothing, able to make life exist where there was none before. Creativity, according to this view, involves a battle, with the blank page and with the author's own laziness and lack of self-discipline (another question at readings: don't you have to be terribly self-disciplined to write a novel?); creativity demands great intellectual vigour and muscular power, the triumphant mastery of matter.

Avoiding this heroic struggle is as bad as cheating at exams; to write autobiographically is to produce an easy version without enough effort being expended, a sort of fake. The verdict? Should try harder. Should attempt to make some real art, and *sweat.* This version's a caricature, of course. But it's the vision of what it means to be an artist that I grew up with and that had a profound impression on me. Well, of course. It might be lovely to believe myself lord and master of creation (you'll notice *lady* and *mistress* don't quite fit in this context), immensely powerful, invincibly strong. This view of the writer is most consoling, like putting on a Superman or Robocop costume for a while, even if in the long run it's done me more harm than good and I've had to discard it. The wrong sort of armour.

You'll remember I spoke of *two* voices, quarrelling. When I listen for and hear the second one, it speaks from an opposite position. This voice insists that art imitates life, that the best art is the most lifelike, that to write fiction is therefore to record what we know, to imitate the real, to copy it lovingly, to produce its exact likeness. A novel, according to this way of thinking, will be praised for its accurate portrayal of adultery amongst the middle classes in Hampstead or unemployment amongst a mining community in Wales, for its authentic dialogue, its realistic details and colouring.

While the first view of writing I described is often seen as real and natural, this second view is the one that gets labelled ideological (though to my mind they're both equally ideological), perhaps because it is often buttressed by a conviction self-declaredly political: that it is *good* to write about lives passed over as uninteresting and unimportant, good to proclaim a hitherto obscured or ignored truth, good to tell it like it is.

The practice of consciousness-raising, for example, among women in feminist groups in the seventies, whereby women struggled to articulate to each other things that had not been said before (so we believed) about our lives, easily became connected to the idea that producing a novel could similarly invoke the vernacular practice of talking to sisters/friends/comrades, opening up in a trusting way, telling all, telling the truth, utilising only that most reliable of narrators: oneself, or a character based on oneself (paradoxically often cast in the third person to disguise her origins and appear objective); a narrator whose impulses were essentially *good.* This kind of connection was made possible because both practices – consciousness-raising and writing stories – involved language. The difference between oral and written language got elided – after all, the citadel of literature was being stormed by the dispossessed. I've given you another caricature, haven't I, and certainly avowedly feminist fiction is characterised by its hostile critics as unsophisticated, artless, ideological, preachy, dull, and, yes, autobiographical. (But a surprising number of people, not only taxi drivers and my brother-in-law, say to me: 'I've had such an amazing life, I've got a few stories to tell, I can tell you, I'd love to write a novel if only I had the time' – it's a common misperception about writing not confined to feminists.) The point I want to make here is that both feminine and feminist writing (writing that supports the status quo and writing that criticises it) have come to be identified, mainly by critics who've read very little of either but who know what they like, with a certain kind of realism that stays within the boundaries of the home and replicates them rather than playing with them. Women writers may be praised and simultaneously subtly blamed or despised for writing about *what we know* – think of the scorn heaped on Anita Brookner's work by a certain sort of critic, or the inferior status given to romances and what are called Aga sagas – though all of these sorts of novels are beloved of the public and sell extremely well. The traditional concerns of women's lives – love and power struggles and money, the great passage rites of puberty, sex, childbirth and death – can still be dismissed as of secondary interest.

When an eminent male writer, in an unguarded moment discussing his selection of books for the best twenty young British novelists promotion was reported as complaining that he couldn't bear the thought of reading one more novel that concerned the onset of menstruation in its heroine (or words to that effect), nobody publicly challenged him. No wonder some women novelists have sought to reclaim the tradition of realist, and by implication autobiographical, writing, and give it a twist, a sting in the tail. Fay Weldon's early novels seized this challenge with relish, serving up plenty of wisdom, anger and wit in the process. Nicole Ward Jouve is another contemporary writer who not only has boldly begun writing literary criticism that declares its autobiographical base but who also writes fiction that experiments with the 'facts' of her own background in Provence, Yorkshire and Massachusetts, even though these are dealt with in an unconventional and modernist fashion. Her work reminds me again of the impossibility of trying to stuff writers into cramped and claustrophobic pigeonholes.

So what happens when a woman writer steps outside them? When she starts to write in a way that cannot be labelled and dismissed as domestic realism? When she enters what's called the realm of the avant-garde and the experimental? What happens is that her gender vanishes. She's perceived as genderless: as writing like a man; as having transcended the merely womanly. She may then become invisible except to her fans, as has been the case with the rigorously modernist work of Christine Brooke-Rose, and as was the case a long time with Angela Carter, whose provocative and brilliant novels proved her not to fit the stereotype of the lady writer. Since Carter didn't hide her sex, her gender, but used it as a springboard for her writing, I think she was seen as a kind of literary monster. Eventually a space was made for her; her greatness was recognised. But before her tragically early death she received only one big literary prize. Women modernists are constantly having to be rescued, re-recognised; as though we only allow a space for one at a time, one per generation.

The fault lies in how we look and what we think we're looking for. Many women writers with aspirations towards creating 'serious' or 'literary' or 'avant-garde' fiction cope with the 'problem' of gender by denying they are women at all. Accepting the denigration of femininity rampant in our culture, they are forced to de-sex themselves to write as they want to. I'm not a woman writer, they characteristically insist: I'm a writer. Who can blame them? If *different* means *worse*, we're all going to rush towards the norm, which remains masculine, though it pretends not to be, but to be bodiless, gender-free.

I gave you just now a bit of a caricature of autobiographical writing of the sort so often combined with domestic realism – its aims, its shortcomings. The main problem I have with it is not its feminist or feminine aspirations but the difficulty of making it work satisfactorily. I discovered this twenty years ago, when I started trying to write short stories and to begin a novel, and I've been rediscovering it ever since. The more I try to do it, the more difficult it becomes. The writing is always being interrupted by something else: a warning siren, a cry of pain, a child's babble, a groan of bliss. These noises off are in the room where I work and also inside me. Their insistent presence, their disruption of the calm smooth surface of my prose, forces me to stop and think about how language works, about what on earth is going on when I try to paint in words a realistic picture of the world I know – or think I know.

I have discovered that language does not function as a simple pane of invisible glass set in a window frame through which I see the real world beyond. Just like oil paint or acrylics or watercolour the glass, the language itself, is matter, material, and conditions how I see the world – to continue with my image, it matters crucially whether the glass is pearly or coloured or opaque, dusty or cracked, thick or thin. And the view depends on where I place myself: leaning far out over the window-sill, half in and half out of my subject matter, or hiding behind a frosted-over glass pane patterned by Jack Frost with sprigs of ferns then pressing a heated penny to it to melt myself a peep-hole.

Having discovered that words are real in themselves I've discovered, with the help of friends who've read Monsieur de Saussure, that as real as wooden signposts words point to things. The word 'chair' is a signpost pointing to the object we've all decided to call a chair. But we might have decided to call a chair a 'jongleridoo'. The signifier, to use the Saussurean term, is not identical with what it signifies; to some extent their connection is arbitrary. Surely here is the amazing power of words: to *seem* so true and so beautiful that using them can seem like having some sort of religious or ecstatic experience, invoking those ancient gods who once dwelt in every aspect of nature and who I think still dwell in words; getting to the deep truth and reality of life, of things; and yet to be at the same time an artefact made by humans, a series of arbitrarily designed signs that can be swapped with one another, muddled up and messed about with like paints or clay, piled up in layers of metaphor, whose meanings slip and change, above all that point at something which is *not there*. The word for the chair is not the chair. The paradox conjured by language: to appear to be so real, to be based on reality, but to be equally concerned with illusion, with theatre, with dance and with play, a show of appearances.

Language is founded upon absence. We don't point with our fingers at the chair in the room beside us; we use a word as pointer to designate the chair that is not there.

Language erupts out of silence and splinters it.

So when I write fiction I'm creating a presence, I'm depending upon the materiality of words to conjure a show of that chair, that person, that relationship she has with the other person glimpsed in the doorway. This presence that fiction creates is crucially connected, I think, with absence, an absence that can be felt as insistently material.

I'll return to this absence and its possible nature a little later on. Here I just want to stress my discovery that writing fiction means using the imagination and cannot mean otherwise, given how language works. Since language cannot mirror 'reality' exactly but helps to create it, any piece of fiction I write which tries to be a replica of the world as it is, the world as it appears to be, on the surface, risks missing the point and failing, because it's not exploiting what language can do. It's stale, flat, dull.

Brought up at school and university to believe in the strict division of categories, that A cannot be B, I've discovered, thanks to the poets whose works lit up my repressed adolescence, the power of metaphor. The rules I grew up with declare that a chair is a chair and that's that. But even as a child, especially as a child, I knew that a chair could be a doll's house, a doll's fortress, a horse for me to ride on, a weapon, a window. An infinite series of meanings opened up. This multiplicity of meanings, of truths, convinces me far more deeply than any single one. Just as words appear to tell the truth and yet make it up, so words tell not one truth but many. Truths: complex, slippery, changeable, fluid. Yet how often we want that not to be so, want to believe in one truth, one God, one leader . . . It can be painful to learn over and over again to rely on uncertainty!

But having discovered that words are always trying to change into their opposites, their myriad and multiple and ambiguous other meanings, so I'm able to realise that I've made a false opposition between writing imaginatively and writing autobiographically. The falsity lies in the division between them, in my use of either/or categories, either/or thinking.

When I'm as truthful as possible (and a little later on I'll indicate why that's so difficult) about what goes on when I'm writing, I feel that autobiography and imagination are deeply connected. Take the word 'invent' for example. I can use this as the opposite of 'I record what I know'. To invent is to be imaginative, to make things up. Yet the Latin *invenio* means I find, I come upon. I find what I know, I discover it. Where do I find it? Inside myself, in that strange space I call the unconscious, the imagination, a place I always experience as interior. And then: I make something up. I make something out of bits, I supply what's missing, the part that's not there. How did I know what to supply, what was lacking? Because it was there once, because I knew it once, before I 'lost' it. That absence again.

Once I stop making rigid separations between sorts of writing, these images of making which connect self and world come flooding up, these images which suggest that self and world are part of each other in a complicated way. Just as writing autobiography requires great art to do it well, so writing imaginatively means opening up to the deep self of the personal unconscious, drawing upon the hidden processes of the psyche, discovering that they can turn into treasures of writing.

Teaching creative writing has helped me to see this. When beginning students, mainly the women, say to me anxiously: oh, I mustn't write about myself or my own experience, that would be self-indulgent and wrong, I invite them to explore that statement by writing their autobiographies, taking no more than twenty minutes, in one hundred words exactly, using the present tense and, very important, using words of only one syllable. The results are always extraordinary examples of surrealism, of *art brut*, and the students are enabled to see how much artifice goes into appearing to tell the truth, how much can be left out, how powerful the artist is to create her illusion of truth. Sometimes the male students have trouble with this exercise precisely because the taboo on writing 'personally' is so strong in them that they don't even know it's there. Similarly, when students insist that they must only write from personal experience or about what they know, I invite them to experiment with what that is. I ask them to think of the worst sin in their own personal code – sleeping with a best friend's husband or committing child abuse or whatever the particular student decides upon – and then to write a short, very short, story in the first person about this sin being committed. In this way a writer discovers a new part of herself she might not have known about before: her nasty, evil side, or at least the side of her that can sympathise with nasty, evil sinners; and so not only is her repertoire of self-knowledge broadened, but she comes into contact with her unconscious – which may include all that she does *not wish* to know about.

It seems to me that *wishing* is indeed an important aspect of the imagination, kick-starting it into life. Perhaps that's a startlingly obvious thing to say, but it's been a revelation to me to discover how many novels which purport to be about something wholly imagined and made up and *other* to the author, in fact, at one level, express what seem to be very strong personal wishes on the author's part. I think it is now more commonly recognised than it used to be that romances are not to be dismissed as 'trash' (a word aimed at their readers, I think, as much as at their content) so much as seen as dramatisations of the acute anxieties afflicting modern women contemplating relationships with men (anticipated or actual readers' ages vary from thirteen to ninety as we know from the example of Dame Barbara Cartland): will he want to get to know me and be intimate? Will he develop into a tender and passionate lover? Will he cherish me in an un-macho way or am I fooling myself? Under his laddish and casual manners is there some real fondness for women, or is there not? Etcetera. These are certainly not questions to be despised, since women need to go on asking them. And the wish at the heart of these novels, that inside every unprepossessing frog *does* lurk a sweet and delicious prince, is absolutely shaped by our culture, which requires such peculiar behaviour on the part of its men and turns its women into detectives hunting for clues: he *seems* cool/indifferent/hasty/emotionally remote, but *perhaps* my love will revive him, warm him and stimulate him into vibrant passionate life? Not very flattering to men, this wish, casting them, in an odd reversal of what you might expect, as Sleeping Beauties hidden behind the thorns of machismo. On a deeper level still, some feminist critics have suggested, the female wish embodied in the romance is that the man actually impersonate the mother and deliver to the swooning heroine all the bliss, all the oceanic feelings she once experienced at the maternal breast and hungers for again. The final kiss, at the book's close, therefore represents not only the mutual orgasm all heterosexual couples are expected to have three times a week, but the ecstatic pleasure of the tiny girl sucking in her mother's milk. Here writer's and reader's imaginations come subversively together. Under its cloak of convention, the romance allows for some disruptive goings on, for the fixed categories of male and female to lurch about a little. Surely that's part of the pleasure and satisfaction offered the reader, albeit unconsciously. The same sort of thing goes on in *Jane Eyre*, where Mr Rochester, the very epitome, we might think, of rampant masculinity, includes cross-dressing in his repertoire and woos Jane on one occasion by disguising himself as a gypsy woman.

Thrillers, similarly, seem to articulate and express their authors' wishes, though the genre allows the wishes to be more deeply hidden in the text. This, on the surface, may apparently concern itself exclusively with police procedures following a murder, with the mean streets of Cardiff or Swansea, of Manchester or Edinburgh, with the low life of north London or Oxford, with the gruesome realities of violent death. On the back of the novel, the blurb tells us about the author, her cottage in the Cotswolds, her comfortable life, devoted husband and golden Labradors; it's clear that she's made her story up, done her research very well, created a totally different world from the one she lives in. And yet, as you read the thriller, the feeling creeps up on you that here, being dramatised, is a passionate wish: for a strong father-figure to lay down the law, set all to rights, bring order out of chaos. A wish for the phallus, indeed. Quite a few of the detectives are good-looking, some are aristocratic. They're *good* men (some even write poetry), not too busy to cook supper for their wives or listen to their teenage children's problems. Some of them are even able to cope with feminists and indeed go so far as to fall in love with them. Thrillers by men, on the other hand, often have cheerily slob-bish detective heroes who have escaped petticoat rule, live on sandwiches, listen to jazz all night if they want to, escape to the pub whenever possible, enjoy sex with good-looking strangers but treat their female colleagues in a completely wonderful and non-sexist way. Thrillers by feminists have something in common with this kind of male thriller. They often dramatise a wish to escape from marriage and domesticity, a wish for adventure. It's compulsory for the heroine to be a rotten cook, have an empty fridge, run or jog or play volleyball to keep herself in the perfect physical condition necessary for chasing villains, to be childless, to be sexually attractive to men without needing to wear makeup or silk lingerie.

We should not despise the novels which embody such wishes. Who amongst us has never ever had even one of them?

You might want to complain, anyway, that these are absurdly reductive readings. Yes, they are. But I've made them in order simply to stress how a piece of writing with a real life and force of its own is strongly rooted in its author's psyche. Good writing, I'm suggesting, gains part of its power from the degree to which it skil-fully articulates its author's unconscious life and wishes. And the writing, of course, makes the writer's unconscious visible to herself. She doesn't write in a trance; she's not a patient on the analyst's couch (for analyst read literary critic or reader); she's aware of her own adventure, to a greater or lesser extent, through the maze of the psyche. She discovers and articulates her wish through the process of mapping it on to the exterior world in language, in symbols. In this process of translation – being carried across, changed into – the symbol may not overtly express the wish but will carry all its emotional charge. We have no need to know the biographical facts of a writer's life in order to understand her work. All we need to do is read her novel as deeply and committedly as possible and let its language, its heaped-up meanings, its symbols, act upon us, both consciously and unconsciously. Then we're not decoding the writer's autobiography, reading it back into the work, but discovering what deep human wish animates the piece of art she has made and set free. We do not need to know, for example, about Charlotte Brontë's unrequited love for her professor in Brussels, Monsieur Héger. The rich network of symbols constructing the narrative of *Jane Eyre* convinces us of a woman's longing to be seen as equal to the man she loves. Jane's passionate cry to Rochester about to equality of their two souls before God moves me because of the language it's written in and because I can respond to it. Charlotte Brontë's wish articulates that of the modern woman reader also.

When a writer tries to create a piece of reality, 'reality as it is', the imagination, that strange internal organ of making, strongly inflects it with meanings to do with the future.

What about the past?

It strikes me, the more I think about it, that the past exerts a terrific pull on our imaginations (not just my own – one of the unspoken assumptions of this essay being that certain psychic processes and experiences are common to all of us as symbol-making creatures who are born and must die); not for nothing did the Greeks name Mnemosyne, memory, as the chief, or mother, of the Muses.

How do I know this? Why do I assert it so confidently?

You remember, I hope, that earlier I mentioned in passing *chaos*, I mentioned *absence*. I want to return to those two words, tug on them, pull some threads together, and start finding my way out of this maze of ideas I've led you into – or, perhaps, more deeply into its heart; which may be the same thing.

A quick digression, first, into the world of visual images.

Over the past few years I've come across, quite by chance, different exhibitions or collections of black-and-white photographs by French photographers representing the daily lives of ordinary working people in the forties, fifties and early sixties in France. I'm ashamed to say I've forgotten the names of the particular photographers; it's the power of the images which has remained and which continues to haunt me. I find the photos – portraits of men and women and children, of young people, of old people – intensely beautiful and moving. Their technical expertise ensures that. I also know that I bring to the photographs my own feelings about what they evoke: a vanished world, a time when agriculture was not heavily industrialised, a time of distinctly local, not international culture, of local customs and festivals and feasts, a way of being characterised by simplicity, affection, innocence . . . No modern horrors are visible in these pictures. The countryside still has hedges and overgrown lanes, there are few motor cars, no TVs or videos, no advertising signs bordering the green fields, no ghetto blasters disturbing the peace.

Stop. This is all sentimental nonsense, isn't it? A dangerous nostalgia. As though all the common forms of cruelty – from rape to wife-beating to incest – weren't going on as usual just outside the frame. I'm saying: things were better then; in the old days; life was simpler, people were good to each other. But why am I saying that? *Why* do these photos move me so, convince me so utterly of their great beauty? What is it about these black-and-white images of a family picnic on the banks of the Seine, a mother and daughter hand in hand by a bridge in Rouen, a mother and daughter posing, smiling, dusters in hand, inside the frame of an ornate mirror?

These images come from the period of my own childhood spent partly in France. They give me back what I have lost – childhood – and enable me to re-create it idealistically as a happy paradise.

They stand in, these images of lost bliss, as images of something even more specific than childhood: she who is paradise itself for the baby, the growing child: the mother.

The power of these photographs comes from their capacity to give me back what I lost, thought I had lost for ever: the maternal body, my mother's body, alive and warm and generous, an image of that body which says that is how she was, that is how we were, once, together. Blissful mutual giving and taking. What the French call *la jouissance* and what the French feminist writers like Julia Kristeva and Hélène Cixous say we find again through writing and reading.

We all have to grow up, we all have to leave paradise. Those are the autobiographical facts. In imagination, we preserve what is precious, we re-enter paradise, or at least we search for it, for the lost mother. In the art we make, we make that lost body, we make it up, we re-make it, we remember it, we re-member it.

Images of destruction here, aren't there? Re-make? Re-member? Has something been destroyed?

What I've let out is the child's anger, the child's fantasies of destruction. The artist's aggression, capacity to destroy.

My myth of speaking and writing (a myth, an explanation on the level of poetry, a psychic 'truth') is that we learn to use language as a kind of birth into absence. The mother, the all-giving breast, is not there: out of terrible feelings of physical pain, rage felt in the body, we learn to say 'I want', to try and summon back the life-giving presence which nourishes us and without which we die. The experience of absence and loss can include our fantasy that we have killed the mother with our angry, hungry wanting. We're left in a pit of despair, abandonment. Into this emptiness comes the desire to make something: the words of desire themselves, images of desire, images of the beloved body we fear we may have destroyed with our biting, wanting, greedy neediness. Out of this *chaos* of feeling, out of this overwhelming sadness at *absence*, we learn to create something beautiful: our words, later on our gifts, later still our works of art. We re-create the mother inside ourselves, over and over again.

There are tremendous taboos laid upon us as adult persons against recovering this knowledge, which is why we tend to mock it. We live in a patriarchy which sentimentalises mothers while it despises them and blames them; whose gods are male. We deny our loss, because it's so painful, for both sexes. Men write more autobiographical memoirs of their fathers, I think, than of their mothers, perhaps partly because they are required to repress the mother in them in order to become masculine. Women can have equal trouble finding an image of sensual loving delight between mother and daughter; the taboo on homosexuality sees to that, it's not just the lived difficulties of that crucial relationship so many of us battle with. Yet we search for the image, try to make one, to make one up. We try to mend what has been broken. We try to make reparation to that lost, broken, but now magically restored body. The taboo ensures we insist that art is all about imagination, has nothing to do with bodily experience, with autobiography!

You'll have heard echoes in what I've been saying of the work of Freud, of Melanie Klein, of contemporary writers on art sympathetic to Klein like Marion Milner, Peter Fuller. Certainly I'm indebted to their work, which has helped me shape my own ideas. But I need to stress the personal aspect of the search. Before reading these writers I was surprised by how everything I wrote went back to maternal loss, maternal absence, and now dares to re-image maternal presence, fullness. I find the theories suggestive, powerfully evocative, 'true', because I've experienced what they're saying inside myself, inside my own work. I hope by now you've forgiven me for talking so much about myself – as the poet Peter Redgrove has said, if we can believe that our own psyche is part of the universe then talking about ourselves is talking about part of the universe – not so greatly to be feared and disapproved of.

I'm suggesting that the place of imagination is at the heart of each of us, at the heart of culture, of society. It's the place inside us where we hold and contain a kind of thinking which re-members how we were as children and still can be: non-rational, wanting to make and give gifts, playful, aggressive, destructive, sad, reparative, joyful. It's a safe place, in which to let go of old certainties, let boundaries dissolve, experience the kind of chaos necessary for new life, new ideas. It's a space we need inside our culture, a space we need to hold our children in, contain them safely in while they fight and learn. If we stay in touch with our own imagination, our own unconscious, our own autobiography, our own childhood, we are more tender towards our own children. We can understand better their aggressive and hating impulses because we know we have felt the same. We won't label them as *either* little angels *or* little devils, because we know that inside us are *both* little angels *and* little devils, both mother and child, both man and woman, both darkness and light, both good and bad. The place of imagination is also perhaps to remind us of the costly effects to our society of either/or thinking, to invite us to a crazy kind of dance inventing some new steps, humming some new kind of music. Artists don't have a premium on this. Each one of us is reaching out to discover that beloved renewed body.

2

On God and *Sans-Permis*

POSTCARD FROM MAYENNE

Independent, June 1994

The landscape of the Mayenne is lush, green and rolling, especially attractive when viewed from the back yard of a second-hand car dealer in the industrial zone of our local town. I spent most of yesterday there, watching the mechanics mend *moto-cyclettes* and tractors and finally get the battery working on my new (second-hand) car.

The best thing about life in France, in my current opinion, is that I, with my twenty-year-old driving phobia and lack of commitment to driving lessons, should have been able to walk into this garage, buy a car, get into it and drive. *Vroom.* I didn't need driving lessons and I haven't got a driving licence. It feels like a miracle.

The car is called a *sans-permis.* Because it's so small and goes at a maximum speed of forty kilometres an hour, its legal status is that of a bike on four wheels. It's automatic, too, and never stalls, so there's none of that terror on hill starts. It simply chugs along until you pull the Stop button and turn it off. A full tank of diesel cost me twenty francs. The *garagiste* couldn't stop laughing. He said to my husband, who'd come along as passenger to supervise my first go at three-point turns outside the bank, 'You are a brave man!'

I don't care if people laugh at me in my tiny car. It's just what I need for building up my confidence in order to believe that one day I will actually pass my driving test and use a 'proper' car. I've broken a self-inflicted and deep-seated taboo: I've always been convinced that I was an idiot with machines and would never be able to drive. Some invisible umbilical cord kept me chained to the house here, dependent on Jim for going anywhere. In London I can travel by bicycle or public transport, but out here, where we live for part of the year, deep in the countryside, you don't go anywhere if you haven't got four wheels. I do bicycle sometimes, but I've got lazier. I need to drive if I'm to see my friends. And it's easier to enter a farmyard and cope with the baying and slavering free-range guard dogs from inside a car. I am a coward in the face of these beasts, and the car will be my armour, like Robocop's.

The mechanic who sold me the car asked: have you driven before? I lied and said no, for the pleasure of seeing him show no disdain. Well, he said: I'll drive you down the road a few kilometres and you drive me back. He indicated the gear-lever: this is Forwards and this is Back. In we got and off we drove. Enormous lorries whizzed past. The mechanic cried: slow down! You're going too fast! I was Mrs Toad: poop poop parp parp.

Tomorrow I shall tootle off to visit my neighbour Madame S. up the road, in her farm where she raises pigs, cows, chickens, ducks and turkeys. She is no stranger to technology: complex milking machinery; portable telephone on her at all times. Her husband rolls home late from the harvesting, on his tractor, these summer nights. Madame S. drives a battered van, very fast. She will smile and shrug at my little car, offer me an *apéritif*, sell me some milk and eggs, instruct me on gardening, restrain her enormous dog while I leap into my *voiturette* and drive home.

Who knows? Next, I might abandon my cherished Olivetti Lettera 22 portable typewriter and race into Le Mans to buy a word processor. I expect out here you can find one that's fully automatic and runs on diesel.

MARY MAGDALENE

by Susan Haskins

Independent on Sunday, 15 September 1992

In the late 1970s I became obsessed with the figure of Mary Magdalene, the follower of Christ who in Gospel legend became the first witness of the Resurrection and who in the cultural tradition was the beautiful repentant whore, a highly coloured version of the eternal feminine. She sprang into life in my imagination as though I'd switched on a strong beam of light and shone it on her. I dreamed of her and heard her voice. An archetype, perhaps a stereotype, had been awakened. I ended up writing a novel about her, which was published in 1984. I made my Mary Magdalene a writer, partly so that she could write a hitherto undiscovered gospel and give my novel an appropriate form, partly so that I could investigate possible links between women's creativity and sexuality. This preamble indicates my special interest in Susan Haskins' book on the saint, since my novel is mentioned therein.

I wasn't alone in being fascinated by the complex and ambiguous image of Mary Magdalene as it's developed over the centuries, of course; other European writers, unknown to me at the time, were also beavering away on novels with similar themes. Mary Magdalene, in yet another of her constant reincarnations, had become very much a woman of our time. Christian feminists were questioning women's oppressed status in the Church. Women in general were admitting to discontent about a Christian heritage of thinking that named men as guardian of the spirit, the intellect, and divided them from the female keepers of the body. Women, named as *the sex*, could feel we lacked souls. As daughters of Eve, we inherited her guilt for introducing sin into the world. The phallus, magically powerful and invisible, was God. It was hard, if you were a woman, to believe you really were created in the image of God. You had to get rid of your body first. Hence the convent-school stress, for girls of my generation growing up in the fifties, on the ideals of feminine purity, chastity, self-denial. Priests preached their celibacy as a negative ideal which kept them from degradation by women. Mary Magdalene erupted into all this pain and muddle, for both sexes, as the very image of the return of the repressed: the numinous body, sexiness and holiness intertwined, God as immanent not transcendent, the desires of the body as sources of religious joy.

I hasten to add that the above represents my view, not that of Susan Haskins. Her book, sober and thoroughly researched cultural history, enacts a conservative and reparative wish: to recover Mary Magdalene from the male fantasists who made her the doyenne of brothels, penitentiaries and more or less tasteful porn, and from the equally abhorrent feminists who made her sex life central to her personality. Susan Haskins equates the two. She rescues Mary Magdalene from the insult of being thought too sexy, very much in the spirit of ladies rescuing fallen women or magdalens in times past, and concludes, it's difficult to avoid thinking, that only a toned-down Magdalene, tidy and discreet and probably celibate, will advance women's cause. What cause is this? Women's quest to be ordained as priests. Ah. Well, one of the most radical feminist views opposing the ordination of women as priests holds that until there's a proper theology recognising the feminine aspect of the Godhead, women priests will be fake men. Certainly, a flaw of Susan Haskins' book is the absence of thorough theological discussion of sex and gender, both historically and recently, from which a consideration of the status of Mary Magdalene can hardly be separated.

En route to its questionable conclusion, the re-establishment of the *true* and *real* figure of the biblical accounts as a good role model for contemporary Christian women, the book is packed with delights. It takes us on a journey through the four Gospels, the way that the early Fathers of the Church developed views of Jesus' teaching, the history of iconography, the narratives of medieval and Renaissance poems and plays, the recently discovered and newly translated Gnostic gospels of Nag Hammadi, Victorian photographic pornography and much more. The figure of Mary Magdalene becomes a lens through which to try and glimpse the prejudices of each century. My reading of all this fascinating material is that Mary Magdalene is a figure of glorious contradictions, embodying one side of the Christian split between the maternal and the sexual; a lost tradition of the indwelling aspect of God; Wisdom or Sophia; and, yes, that corrupted figure of sex fantasy. Surely this is the point. To rescue the Magdalene as a figure of autonomous loving discipleship needn't mean disavowing the poets' and painters' delight in portraying her beauty. Is it only sexist imaginations that equate the virgin (she who walks by herself) with the whore (she who belongs to no man)? Part of the Magdalene's appeal is her challenge to these either/or categories. In the world of the unconscious, virgin and whore dance together, friends. Christianity tried to separate them. Recently they're getting back together again.

In the end I think Mary Magdalene *is* her myth. We can't take out the true bits and chuck the false bits. Well, we can if we believe in the Author, that one who dictated the Bible and knew just what He was up to. If we believe in lots of scribes and seers, some of them female, then we can cherish a whole kaleidoscope of Magdalenes, a heavenly host of sexy female saints.

THE PLACE OF WOMEN IN THE CATHOLIC CHURCH: ON THE NEW ROMAN CATHOLIC CATECHISM

Independent, 10 August 1994

The catechism I knew as a child aged eleven studying in confirmation class was a small blue booklet whose questions and answers we chanted aloud just as we did our tables. The parish priest popped into our classroom in the convent school to make sure we had got it right. 'Who made you?' 'God made me.' 'Why did God make you?' 'To know, love and serve him in this life and to be happy with him for ever in the next.' Simple certainties dulled by repetition. I don't remember ever being required to discuss the faith I professed in singsong. It was poetry to be recited. Praise if you got it right. Then came the Ecumenical Council called Vatican II, the gales of change sweeping through the Church, blowing away repressive traditions in favour of renewal. Some called it the work of the Holy Spirit, others feared it as revolution. The Church tried to engage with the modern world, to support the oppressed, to imagine a theology which could celebrate and include lay virtues. Formerly heretical questions about the goodness of sex, the potential of women, the contribution of homosexuals, the injustice of labour laws and wage differentials, began to be asked, though perhaps not in Rome.

Now we have a new catechism which distances itself from these developments in many ways. I say 'we' though I lost my faith over twenty years ago, easily, for the simple feminist reason, that I could no longer bear sitting in silence listening to male priests telling me how to feel and think. I think now it was easier to be that child of eleven with her small blue booklet and boring certainties. This new compendium of the faith weighs in at nearly 700 pages and employs appeals to reason and understanding to persuade the Catholic reader that the priestly authorities do have a hotline to Him Up There and that they are right. This is theology of the scholastic, classifying, nit-picking and ultimately tub-thumping kind. If you don't agree with it that just proves how deluded and corrupted you are and it's your own fault. Sin, you see, is *your* willed decision, *your* choice to turn away from God. It's quite difficult to argue against nearly 700 pages of rhetorical statements pretending to be arguments for your own good. I was certainly reminded, reading through this tome, of the hectoring voice of the parish priest of my childhood, he who was convinced he spoke for God and took his time telling us why. Only now I am a fast aggressive reader who can skip pages; I didn't learn *that* at convent school. There, we knew that the Author *was* God.

This new catechism, the apparently much-needed update of the last one, produced in the sixteenth century, implacably reinstates theology as a runthrough of fixed ideological positions masquerading as eternal verities. In the sixties, seventies and eighties, theology flirted with poetry, with psychoanalysis, with political jargon, even with feminism, those human constructs. But now we're back to what the good guys always knew was true and knew was best for us. Take, for example, the symbolic meaning of Christ's death on the Cross. The new theology suggested that the Crucifixion provided an image of a God who was putting patriarchy to death, who was the God of the second chance, the God of the damaged, the oppressed, the weak, those who are broken and make mistakes, those who cannot be macho and don't want to be. The new catechism, on the other hand, takes us back to the traditional doctrine of the Atonement: we, as human beings, are in our nature so fallen, so evil, so alienated, that God had to put his son on the Cross to rescue us. I repudiate this doctrine with all my heart, as one that damages and stunts children's moral, psychological and emotional growth. What a start in life, to grow up believing, as I did, that you are responsible for Christ's agonising death. A double burden of guilt if you are female, since we all know the gender of the one lusting after food and knowledge in the garden of Eden and so setting the whole sorry caravan of blame and self-hate in motion.

Sin is necessary to the writers of this catechism, perhaps because if their readers can be convinced of their sinfulness they will be equally persuaded of their need for priestly advice and absolution. Goodness and virtue are discussed in vague terms such as 'charity' or 'growth towards perfection', but sin takes up quite a few column inches, requires quite a bit of defining. Sin itself, if you believe in a personal God, is well defined as a loss of that God, a turning away from him (the guys have repudiated all feminine language for their Supreme Person), but the list of ways to turn away makes fascinating reading. It's hard not to think of a sin supermarket, where you pick 'n' mix the sins that suit or attract. I'd agree with the guys, for example, that rape certainly qualifies as a sin and child abuse too, but then on the other hand I cannot agree that homosexuality should be listed next to rape, that incest be put on the same level as two unmarried people having a love affair. But such is the mad logic of the current bosses of the Church in sexual matters. Only one sex act qualifies as good: sex between married partners intending to procreate. It's laughable that the fantasies of celibate men should prescribe the sexual behaviour of woman, who are the ones that bear the babies and are often left holding them. It's even more laughable that these earnest clerics heartily disapprove of fantasy and consider pornography a sin, since not only does it voyeuristically reveal intimate acts best kept secret but it seduces us to prefer illusion to reality. What is the attitude of the Church to sex if not illusion? Celibate guys are notoriously idealistic about sex, assuring us that every encounter is about total giving of the self, total union, total spiritual growth. What about comic and absurd sex? What if you don't come? Is that a sin? Certainly, coming *too often* seems to constitute a sin. Why on earth should God, if God is a person (which I doubt), not enjoy the thought of her creatures coming and laughing? The Catholic Church, it has to be said, had a bad start on sex. Not only its pagan and Greek influences but the state of scientific knowledge of the day was against it. If you didn't know the role of female ovulation in conception, it was easier to imagine a masculine god who did everything all by himself. The Virgin was a flower-bed in which he planted his seed; thus women cannot be actively creative and procreative; thus there is no need for God to be Mother too. The new catechism implicitly repeats all this. Becoming a parent involves the chance, it solemnly intones, to share in the Fatherhood of God. Imagine a woman in labour crying out: now at last I experience the Fatherhood of God! It doesn't quite work. But the catechism struggles on, saying 'Man' as though it were a neutral word like 'Umbrella' to cover both sexes. 'Woman', here, is a wife, a helper and support to Man. That is what equality means. It is quite possible that whole convents of nuns helped to draft or question this document but their influence does not show. That's it, ladies. Now please get back to cleaning the church, and remember, if you have a paid job, that strikes are often sinful and profits necessary. Abortion, of course, according to this view, cannot even be discussed as a necessary evil: it constitutes a crime against this God with no understanding of the complexity of human relationships, their power imbalances and yearnings; this God with no appreciation whatsoever of the unpredictability of the unconscious, the fact that we are not solely rational, responsible and in control. Where the new theology tried to come to terms with this, to understand how painful and difficult it is to accept ourselves as forever good-and-bad, dark-and-light, the new catechism slams us back into the simplistic thinking that comforted me as an eleven-year-old. It will disappoint generations of Catholics who had begun to dare to work out their own morality, to listen to their own hearts alone and in community.

THE FLESH MADE WORD

Broadcast on Radio 3, 27 July 1997

The Christian Church has traditionally argued that God is a being completely different from us: a spirit who's invisible, without edges or shape, dwelling above human creatures in a heaven perceived as Up There, the top layer in the sandwich. God was thought of as male, which may have made sense during centuries of masculine dominance. God was named as Master, King, Lord, Law-Giver, Judge, because those were the jobs performed by men of the ruling classes. Men were for a long time thought to have more soul than women, who thus became despised as bodies who symbolised all that these would-be powerful men were frightened of: decay, change, imperfection, chaos, sex and death. In short, the human condition.

It's a story that's become clearer and more transparent to us as it's become criticised. Women are supposedly burdened by our bodies and by our role as child bearers and rearers; we are less rational, intellectual and spiritual than men; we stand in need of much firmer religious guidance. And so on. Nowadays, many men are prepared to admit to feeling just as insulted by this partial and prescriptive view as women do. Change is in the air. For example, women can even be priests now, in part of the Christian Church. Surely, the bad old days of female subjugation are over; the battle's been won.

Not quite. I don't think that simply adding female figures to our panoply of images for God – calling God Mother as well as Father, for example – is quite enough; even though for many, this is going too far. (If you can't bring yourself to accept that God could be Mother, though, it just shows in what low esteem you hold mothers.) No, the simple switching or adding of names just disguises the problem. Christians still talk of priests and women priests; they still expect women priests to wear dog collars, that ridiculous masculine accessory. Women still have to play down their femaleness in order to be accepted. Can you imagine the Anglicans rejoicing over a band of priestesses, sexy, glamorous, maternal, dressed in red silk? Er, no. Dog collars and dowdy clothes, please. No *décolletage* or high heels.

The contradictions around women are still in place. Femaleness gets hidden out of sight in the interests of equality, and difference gets invoked only to cope with issues the Church finds troublesome, like female sexuality. The body, particularly the female body, has remained a problem. Oh yes, I know theologians insist that the human body is sacred, but I don't believe they really think that. They forgive the body for existing by saying it is the envelope of the soul. The body is bearable because necessary, like a sort of carriage, to get us through life and into heaven. The Church goes into frenzies of anxiety about how the body should be corralled by moral laws. Nothing too messy, please! The sort of body the Church can cope with is like the kind of baby recommended by Victorian experts on childcare: tidy, clean, smiling, *controlled*. There are bodily processes the Christian religious tradition would find it impossible to let us think of as sacred: bodies that retch, leak, menstruate, piss and shit, vomit, come ecstatically, are not supposed to exist inside a church and are generally not welcome. Charismatic services, which seem to induce this kind of uncontrolled Dionysiac body, are viewed with suspicion by many Church authorities. Even laughter doesn't go down that well.

The point is, that if you ban the body, if you repress it and squash it down, it will return, it will rise up, burst forth in ways that may distress you and outrage or puzzle others. Too many priests, vowed to a celibacy that was in fact based on misogyny, have taken out their angry neediness on the bodies of female parishioners, of children in their pastoral care. Too many nuns, taught to fear and despise their own sexuality, have taken out their rage and rebellion on the girls they are supposed to be educating. Yes, of course there are some good, holy monks, nuns and priests who can make the vow of celibacy something joyful and loving, but for those of us who grew up in the Catholic Church, as I did, there are all too many figures in authority who have quite clearly been damaged by a teaching that can't value the body and blames its own problem on the opposite sex.

One way that the repressed body returns, passionately and magnificently, in the Catholic tradition – or perhaps despite it – is through art. The visual image fuses body as symbol with body as reality. Take the thousands and thousands of paintings of Mary Magdalene made over the last two thousand years, and see how gloriously she embodies the female body touched by divinity. Officially, in the hysterical Catholic theology which splits body from soul, mother from whore, she is the *repentant* whore – it's difficult to be a Catholic saint who is both holy and actively sexual – but when you look at these images for any length of time you realise how Mary Magdalene is the missing half – the sexual half – of the Virgin Mary, the Mother of God. Take the two women, put them back to back, join them up again, and you've got a whole saint: passionate, maternal, sexy, visionary. The Church can't allow that. To control women it slices us down the middle.

But the artists reached for a deeper, taboo, unspoken truth.

Their Magdalenes do not suggest repentent fallen women nearly so much, as they dream of a spirituality reintegrated with corporeality. The fact that they are painted according to voyeuristic rules – bosoms peeping over hair shirts, flashes of thigh, abandoned postures, strings of pearls in one hand and skulls in the other – only gives the viewer more clues that something contradictory and unconscious is going on. The great thing about the Catholic tradition is that, though it oppresses women horribly by naming them as semi-devils, it simultaneously gives them a visible place, unlike Protestantism which simply ignores them. Femininity is so powerfully contradictorily present in the Catholic Church that you *can't* ignore it. Once you get over your rage at being blamed for the Fall of Man, you can start to enjoy the bizarre ways in which women are represented in religious culture and what this suggests about women's perceived relationship to God. Mary Magdalene is clearly able, according to the artists, to imagine an erotic contact with God. There is a long tradition in literature, which comes down to us alongside the paintings, of female mystics claiming that their direct access to the divine gave them experiences of bliss, which they often described as heat, sweetness and light, or in images of wedding nights, which to a modern reader sounds just like descriptions of passionate, happy, fulfilled sex. Some modern critics get very angry with these mystics, very scornful, and assert that, poor deluded hysterically repressed dears, they were just engaging in wish-fulfilment and imagining the heterosexual love-making denied them by their vows as nuns.

I wonder is it that simple? The anger that medieval priests expressed towards female mystics who contacted God directly without the intervention of the Church's rules and rituals sounds suspiciously like the anger of some post-Freudians insisting that the only valid female orgasm is the vaginal one produced by socially sanctioned heterosexual intercourse. Yesterday's mystics become today's lesbian mothers. Doing it their own way. Beyond the pale. An orgasm by any other name would feel as sweet? The issue's one of control. The body finds ways to experience bliss, and the experience of bliss can be named as an experience of God. This seems to anger two lots of people: the atheists who insist that mystical rapture is a hysterical substitute for real sex, and the religious fundamentalists who insist that sexual pleasure has no contact with the divine.

But isn't the body marvellously democratic, wonderfully cutting down hierarchies and slashing through either/or thinking? Because the body comes, weeps, cries out, thrashes about, hungers, is sated – *that*'s the truth, however we choose to interpret it. Our tears of despair and sorrow are exactly the same tears as our tears of joy. The orgasm produced by the hurly-burly of the *chaise-longue* is the same experience as the orgasm produced by the deep deep peace of the marriage bed – it's we who insist on giving them separate and different significances.

We are our bodies and what is sacred is our capacity to make symbols of our bodily life. The numinous consists not in looking upwards, denying our bodily existence, but looking outwards and inwards, rejoicing in it, celebrating it.

God's hidden. God's come down from the sky and become part of us. The Christian myth takes us so far and no further: God became Man, in Jesus Christ. Now we have to lurch on again. I reject the doctrine of the Atonement, that because of my sinfulness God-as-Man died an unspeakably hideous death on the Cross. (Sorry, but I refuse to be saddled with that responsibility; I was born needy and crying out, hungry, even raging perhaps, but also, certainly, loving; I am not Fallen, I am just human – I am not wicked.) I've now ended up wondering whether God isn't inside *everybody*, not just Jesus Christ.

We don't know, most of us, that we've got God inside us. We don't dare imagine it. We don't want it. It might be too much for us. Especially if we think of that old God, the Judge and Law-Giver, the Blamer and Punisher, what Freudians call the Super-Ego – well, who wants that sort of God inside them? Like some old killjoy peeking in just as you're starting to have a good time and ruining all your fun.

I don't mean that kind of God (or his deputy the Virgin Mary in her role as policewoman whom we were taught about at convent school: watch out girls she can see *everything* you do) because I've stopped thinking of God as a person. Those images belong to certain periods of our history. First of all, it seems clear now from the archaeological evidence, we used to think of God as a mother, and worshipped the Goddess under her different aspects and ages, her waxing and waning like the moon between life and death. At this time, men's role in reproduction probably wasn't known; it seemed as though women produced children all by themselves; no wonder they were regarded as gods. The succeeding culture of father-right swung the other way: ovulation wasn't discovered until relatively recently, so the myth grew up that fathers did it all by themselves. The Christian myth officially records this. God the Father impregnates the Virgin Mary with God the Son. God in this scenario has to be male: the divine sperm is what counts; the woman's body is merely a seedbed.

Christian iconography intriguingly depicts both the approved version of the myth and its underside. Pictures of the male God's sperm, disguised as a dove, shooting into Mary's vagina, disguised as her ear, are very common. That was supposed to depict the Word being made flesh: the Logos substituted for the penis, becoming the phallus, and became fantastically important: what men said was *correct* and *true*; they were the creators, the makers. By sleight of hand, women were deprived of creative power and of speech.

Well, that was one way of looking at it. Because the artists were able to access the unconscious, and the God hidden deep therein, as rhythms of inspiration and creativity, they were able to come up with ambiguous, suggestive, inexplicable images that refuse to be neat mirror images of the official portraits of the dominant religious culture.

I'm thinking here of a painting like Piero della Francesca's *Madonna del Parto*, surely one of the most beautiful and powerful, sexy and numinous paintings of the Christian era – which represents the pregnant Virgin underneath a canopy whose raised edges are held by angels. The painting evokes female divinity through acceptance of maternity, just as in the old folkloric images the Goddess could be worshipped throughout Europe as a pregnant woman. Piero's Madonna fuses and reintegrates the physical and the divine: her swelling body is both the image of fertility, fecundity, hope and faith in the future; and also the symbol of the body as interior space, the site of the imagination, God's dark pavilion. The angels drawing back the curtains which shelter her tell us this. The angels have come from inside her; they are her dreams, her inspiration, her as yet unborn words, her poems, her paintings. Her hand parts the slit in her dress and pauses inside. She tells us that the interior life matters, and can be mapped on to the exterior world. The angels exist both inside and outside her. Here's an end to that traditional splitting between inside world – female – and outside world – male. Piero's woman is both maternal and sexy, both connected and free, both queenly and ordinary. She moves between the conscious and unconscious domains, and links them. Bringing God into the light of day, she demonstrates to us how we can find God in darkness, in our own unconscious.

The old mother goddesses, officially cast out by the masculine religion of Christianity with its drama of Father and Son, survived in pagan practices, in the folklore and heresies that have always flourished at the fringes. The female body, so feared and repressed, returns to haunt and dazzle us in the shapes of visionaries and visions – the Virgin Mary, apparently increasingly making herself visible all over the world in our own day, seems to represent, to those who see her or are moved by reports of her presence, Godness itself. God is presented as female form. There is clearly a tremendous hunger among people to have bodily experiences of God: why else do miraculous statues bleed and weep? Here are those physical processes shunned by the Church: menstruation, lactation, newly made numinous and holy. The reality of these miraculous events and visions is a psychic one. People produce and project their own images, individually and communally. God is worshipped through images of the physical. God is found through images of the physical. God is not any longer simply Him Up There. God has become part of us.

We can't go back to the days of the old mother goddesses, which belonged to a certain time, a certain culture. Similarly, as patriarchy falls apart and decays, its day over, then the old certainty of God as Father Superior starts to rock and shake. But if God isn't Mum or Dad, then who or what?

For me it's enough that mystics, artists and poets suggest that God is incarnate in all creation, no longer transcendent but immanent. This in fact is an old tradition. Mystics at the edge of acceptability, warily skirting heresy and being burnt at the stake in punishment, have spoken for centuries of personal experience of fusion with the divine as a physical reality. Theirs is a theology that includes all of us. Each of us is born creative. Each of us participates in the Creation, the dance and flow of atoms of which the modern physicists speak, which goes on *now*, isn't over once and for all. Each of us can join in making and remaking the world, feel part of the whole.

When that happens – that experience of blissful 'inner' connectedness with the 'outside' world, the universe, of which the mystics speak – then God becomes what links us all together, animals and humans and rocks and plants. God is the force that grows us and wants us to flourish. God is our eating and drinking and gardening and love-making. God is the energy in our bodies, their knowledge and suffering and love.

Perhaps names for God are less nouns than verbs. God is a shorthand for the astonishing and complex processes of the world of which we are part – not observing it but belonging in it – and when we bring God down to earth that releases us into joining the artists and the scientists, the painters and the poets, and all the people who are talking to one another in new languages they themselves invent.

3

On Certain Writers

THE PASSIONATE READER: *POSSESSION* AND ROMANCE

Talk given at Birkbeck College, London, 3 June 1991

To begin with. To begin at the end. Very close to the ending of *Possession*, here's the omniscient narrator (just one of many narrative voices weaving the story of this densely textured novel) musing on the power and pleasure that reading brings to Roland, the book's contemporary hero:

> It is possible for a writer to make, or remake at least, for a reader, the primary pleasures of eating, or drinking, or looking on, or sex. Novels have their obligatory *tour-de-force*, the green-flecked gold omelette *aux fines herbes*, melting into buttery formlessness and tasting of summer, or the creamy human haunch, firm and warm, curved back to reveal a hot hollow, a crisping hair or two, the glimpsed sex. They do not habitually elaborate on the equally intense pleasure of reading . . . And yet, natures such as Roland's are at their most alert and heady when reading is violently yet steadily alive . . .
>
> There are readings – of the same text – that are dutiful, readings that map and dissect, readings that hear a rustling of unheard sounds, that count grey little pronouns for

> pleasure or instruction and for a time do not hear golden or apples. There are personal readings, that snatch for personal meanings, I am full of love, or disgust, or fear, I scan for love, or disgust, or fear. There are – believe it – impersonal readings – where the mind's eye sees the lines move onwards and the mind's ear hears them sing and sing.
>
> Now and then there are readings which make the hairs on the neck, the non-existent pelt, stand on end and tremble, when every word burns and shines hard and clear and infinite and exact, like stones of fire, like points of stars in the dark – readings when the knowledge that we *shall know* the writing differently or better or satisfactorily, runs ahead of any capacity to say what we know, or how. In these readings, a sense that the text has appeared to be wholly new, never before seen, is followed, almost immediately, by the sense that it was *always there*, that we the readers, knew it was always there, and have *always known* it was as it was, though we have now for the first time recognised, become fully cognisant of, our knowledge.

Shortly after this, Roland, in the best tradition of the *Bildungsroman*, discovers that he is, after all, not just a scholar of literature, but also a poet: 'He had time to feel the strangeness of before and after; an hour ago there had been no poems, and now they came like rain and were real.' At this point my own tears came like rain – I wept with pleasure at Roland's release and my own, the bliss of having so many words handed to me.

It's because I had such pleasure reading *Possession* that I'm writing this. I want to offer you my reading of this novel in the hope that it may meet yours, speak to it. Mine is just one reading among thousands, and these thousands of readings are encouraged by *Possession* itself, its structure and content so deeply and playfully committed to exploring questions of authorship and authority, interpretation and intertextuality, pastiche and plagiarism. *Possession* is a novel which, while it invites the reader to make it up, invent it, with each new reading, simultaneously resists being reduced to one line of argument, one ideological position, one kind of suggestion. It's too artful and tricksy, too knowing, for that. Its narrators are ahead of us at every turn, teasing us, outwitting us. If in this essay I offer a reading of *Possession* which ends up discussing what the novel omits, what it discards, what it represses, I know that I stand already rebuked by the text itself. Listen, for example, to this interchange between the two scholars of literature, Beatrice Nest and Maud Bailey. Beatrice is speaking:

> 'A Professor Stern came. From Tallahassee. She wanted to know – to know – to find out about Ellen Ash's sexual relations – with him – or anyone. I told her there was nothing of that kind in this journal. She said there must be – in the metaphors – in the omissions. We were not taught to do scholarship by studying primarily what was omitted, Dr Bailey. No doubt you find me naive.'

Maud replies:

> she may have been right. Maybe what you find baffling is a systematic omission—'
>
> Beatrice thought. '*That* I may grant. Something is omitted. I fail to see why it must be presumed to be – that kind of thing.'

Maud admits:

> 'I agree, Dr Nest. In fact I do agree. The whole of our

> scholarship – the whole of our thought – we question everything except the centrality of sexuality – Unfortunately feminism can hardly avoid privileging such matters. I sometimes wish I had embarked on geology myself.'

The irony here, of course, is that we discover that Ellen Ash's journal *does* conceal facts of a sexual sort, does deny knowledge of a sexual sort, in two ways: Ellen does not write of her terror of sex and her refusal to consummate her marriage with her husband, nor does she admit to knowing about his love affair with the poet Christabel LaMotte. So, inspired by the energetic Professor Stern and her insatiable curiosity about other people's sexual relations, here I shall allow myself what Byatt calls 'the primary pleasure of . . . looking on', the childish pleasure of the voyeur, also perhaps the pleasure of the geologist (such as Maud claimed she should have been and Randolph Ash of course was): I'm going to dig away at part of the surface of the novel's text and discover (make up, invent) some of what's buried underneath it: fossils, a lost fairy kingdom, unuttered words, and yes, even sex.

I'm going to do this by taking seriously *Possession*'s claim, in its subtitle, to be *a romance.* I want to find out what strength it draws from the romance genre, whether it offers its readers similar pleasures, whether it subverts the genre in any way, whether it offers a traditional happy ending. What myth does *Possession* criticise and enact? What other myths does it reject?

Nowadays, the term 'romance' denotes a particular narrow genre of popular fiction associated, in this country, with the publishers Mills & Boon and aimed at a specifically female readership. But as Ann Rosalind Jones points out in her essay 'Mills and Boon meets feminism' (1986):

> romance has been a persistently popular mode in western literature: lovers have met, separated and been blissfully reunited since Alexandrian Greece, as in Longus' *Daphnis and Chloe*, in the Roman comic theatre, in Arthurian cycles, Italian pastoral, and throughout the popular as well as now canonized psychological/realist novels of the eighteenth and nineteenth centuries. But it is only recently that romance has been aimed so exclusively at women. It was written and read by aristocrats of both sexes until the eighteenth century; only then did it begin to be mocked as a feminine preoccupation.

Jean Radford, in her introduction to the same volume of essays (*The Progress of Romance*, 1986), makes the point the other way round:

> It is possible to argue about 'romance' . . . that the only continuity is in the term: that there is no historical relationship between Greek 'romances', medieval romance, Gothic bourgeois romances of the 1840s, late nineteenth-century women's romances and mass-produced romantic fiction now – except the generic term. In so far as genres are contracts between a writer and his/her readers, these contracts, and the conventions which go with them, obviously differ according to the conditions of class, ideology and literacy in different social formations. Yet it is possible, I think, to give some weight to the claim that romance is one of the oldest and most enduring of literary modes which survives today.

Possession, as a self-conscious postmodernist text with a great sense of humour, energetically draws upon this rich literary tradition and eclectically mixes motifs and themes from different periods. To read this novel is to step into a magical world in which reason gives way to imagination, the normal sense of time is suspended, and history seems to run both backwards and forwards, an enchanted kingdom in which narrative is a golden web going forwards, backwards and sideways, ensnaring us and holding us spellbound. Ancient Breton folk tales, for example, rewoven and retold by the peasant woman Gode in the nineteenth century to the future novelist Sabine de Kercoz and her cousin the poet Christabel LaMotte, resurface in both women's later writings and conversation and again in Byatt's fictional version of twentieth-century feminist literary criticism. The characters' fictions, and their lives, overlap and mingle, just as the present does with the past. Roland and Maud, in pursuit of the secrets concealed/revealed by the Ash–LaMotte correspondence, are lured by the power of the two poets' words (criss-crossing, looping back and forth) into stepping beyond the conventions of their lives so far into a new space where they will be utterly changed. Maud has written on the concept of thresholds, of liminality, in LaMotte's poetry; now she has to cross her own self-imposed boundaries and wait to discover what happens next without being in control of it. She doesn't know consciously what's going on; the reader does, through attending to the play of images which structures the text. For example, Roland, using Maud's bathroom for the first time, when he visits her in Lincoln to ask for her help in quest, notes that it's 'a chill green glassy place glittering with cleanness, huge dark green stoppered jars on water-green thick glass shelves, a floor tiled in glass tiles into whose brief and illusory depths one might peer, a shimmering shower curtain like a glass waterfall, a blind to match, over the window, full of watery lights'.

The reader immediately remembers that green is a colour beloved also of the nineteenth-century Christabel, she who wears little green boots just like Maud's and, moreover, invents the drowned underwater kingdom of Is in her epic poem, she who writes of the fairy/monster Melusina lying, beautiful and voluptuous, in her great marble bath, swishing her thick fish's tail, she who experiences, with Ash, on their brief clandestine visit to the north, the magic and power of waterfalls. Later in the novel, Roland kneels at the keyhole of another bathroom, to discover whether or not Maud is using it, whether or not he can go in; he's caught by Maud, as she emerges half-naked, the touch and sight of her dazzling white limbs providing his *coup de foudre*. The reader immediately remembers the husband of Melusina in the folk tale, he who spies upon his fairy wife through the bathroom keyhole and is punished for it. Roland, however, isn't so lightly written off: his name gives us our first clue that he is a true hero – 'Childe Roland to the dark tower came' – and he pops up, I think, in one of Christabel's stories as the Childe who meets the three whiteladies and has to choose between them, *whitelady* being of course *a fairy* but also an image, often evoked, for both Maud and Christabel, both white-fleshed, both initially perceived as proudly asexual: spinster, celibate; whiteness as purity.

This one example of word-play must stand for the way in which the whole of *Possession* engages in a dance of metaphors Shakespearian in its richness, wit and profundity. Juggling with metaphors in this way, the romance here functions as a game which allows the reader all the fun of believing she herself plots all her moves; it functions as a thriller does, soliciting the active participation of the reader, encouraging her repeatedly to try and work out what will happen next even as it sweeps her off her feet and on with the chase. In this way the reader is given two pleasures: the pleasure romance traditionally offers of safe seduction – being able to lie back and be carried away by the story, knowing it will all turn out all right in the end, that boy will find girl again and live happily ever after with her – and the pleasure of having to sit up and take note of where you're going, note the undermining of that plot, the dangerous seduction – *will* it turn out all right, aren't things rather more complicated (look at all those metaphors) than that? Both these pleasures of reading link the reader into the heterosexual coupling at the core of romance; behind them is another pleasure reaching further back, to earlier sensual-erotic experience: confident in the omniscience and delightful power of the narrator who holds all the other narratives together, who cradles all the characters, all the jokes, all the leaping words in her firm embrace, the reader is held as a baby is held by its mother, fed with blissful words and stories, over and over again, as much and as often as she wants, the odd burp or hiccup only adding to the fun. It seems to me that by evoking the narrative pleasures of romance – the greed for more, the hunger to reach the end, the drive towards satiety and bliss – *Possession* assures its readers of one of the deepest pleasures there is: a pleasure we believe we have lost, as we have lost infancy. This romance returns us to it. I hope I've indicated that the reiteration of this early pleasure (romance narrative as good milk) is only the foundation for the other, altogether more adult and more sophisticated delights offered by this novel.

I'm beginning to sound like Leonora Stern. At least, she's probably the only character in *Possession* who would view reading a romance in these terms. Not that I can claim too much credit in spotting those linked motifs, those thrilling correspondences, I mentioned earlier. In a novel which enjoys itself discussing the process of creation as much as this one does, which teases the reader with the illusion that she can make of the novel what she will, credit has to go to the author, that serenely jovial figure who's constantly getting her narrators to joke that she doesn't exist, who keeps deconstructing herself in her text only to pop up elsewhere. Certainly it's not the would-be clever reader who discovers she's part of a romance; the characters themselves acknowledge their indebtedness to the genre. Sabine de Kercoz, for example, writes in her journal (her own piece of fiction, as she admits, about her bewitching cousin) of the talk she has with Christabel on writing:

> She talked of *Melusina* and the nature of epic. She wants to write a Fairy Epic, she says, not grounded in historical truth, but in poetic and imaginative truth – like Spenser's *Faerie Queene*, or Ariosto, where the soul is free of the restraints of history and fact. She says Romance is a proper form for women. She says Romance is a land where women can be free to express their true natures, as in the Ile de Sein or Síd, though not in this world.
>
> She said, in Romance, women's two natures can be reconciled. I asked, which two natures, and she said, men saw women as double beings, enchantresses and demons or innocent angels.
>
> 'Are all women double?' I asked her.
>
> 'I did not say that,' she said. 'I said all men see women as double. Who knows what Melusina was in her freedom with no eyes on her?'

Roland, the modern hero in search of scholarly truth, has mixed feelings about being caught up in romance:

> Roland thought, partly with precise postmodernist pleasure, and partly with a real element of superstitious dread, that he and Maud were being driven by a plot or fate that seemed, at least possibly, to be not their plot or fate but that of those others. And it is probable that there is an element of superstitious dread in any self-referring, self-reflexive, inturned postmodernist mirror-game or plot-coil

> that recognises that it has got out of hand, that connections proliferate apparently at random, that is to say, with equal verisimilitude, apparently in response to some ferocious ordering principle, not controlled by conscious intention, which would of course, being a good postmodernist intention, *require* the aleatory or the multivalent or the 'free', but structuring, but controlling, but driving, to some – to what? – end. Coherence and closure are deep human desires that are presently unfashionable. But they are always both frightening and enchantingly desirable. 'Falling in love', characteristically, combs the appearances of the world, and of the particular lover's history, out of a random tangle and into a coherent plot. Roland was troubled by the idea that the opposite might be true. Finding themselves in a plot, they might suppose it appropriate to behave as though it was that sort of plot. And that would be to compromise some kind of integrity they had set out with.

Quite soon afterwards Roland becomes resigned to being a character in a story:

> Maud was County, and he was urban lower-middle-class, in some places more, in some places less acceptable than Maud, but in almost all incompatible.
>
> All *that* was the plot of a Romance. He was in a Romance, a vulgar and a high Romance simultaneously, a Romance was one of the systems that controlled him, as the expectations of Romance control almost everyone in the Western world, for better or worse, at some point or another.
>
> He supposed the Romance must give way to social

realism, even if the aesthetic temper of the time was against it.

In any case, since Blackadder and Leonora and Cropper had come, it had changed from Quest, a good romantic form, into Chase and Race, two other equally valid ones.

Early on in the novel, Roland, reads the journal of the dead Ellen Ash, her account of reading Christabel's romance Melusina and how wonderful she found it:

> My recent reading has caused me for some reason to remember myself as I was when a young girl, reading high Romances and seeing myself simultaneously as the object of all knights' devotion – an unspotted Guenevere – and as the author of the Tale. I wanted to be a Poet and a Poem, and now am neither . . .
>
> I hit on something I believe when I wrote that I meant to be a Poet and a Poem. It may be that this is the desire of all reading women, as opposed to reading men, who wish to be poets and heroes, but might see the inditing of poetry in our peaceful age, as a sufficiently heroic act. No one wishes a man to be a Poem . . . But I now think – it might have been better, might it not, to have held on to the desire to be a Poet? I could *never* write as well as Randolph, but then no one can or could, and so it was perhaps not worth considering as an objection to doing something.
>
> Perhaps if I had made his life more difficult, he would have written less, or less freely. I cannot claim to be the midwife to genius, but if I have not *facilitated*, I have at least not, as many women might have done, *prevented*. This is a very small virtue to claim, a very negative achievement to hang my whole life on.

Yet Ellen's journal, lengthily quoted, shows her to have been at the very least a competent writer, if an unpublished one, and her capacity to *plot*, to manipulate others, to conceal evidence, provides the pivot on which the book's denouement turns. To live inside romantic dreams (in this case Ellen's wish to believe in her own perfect marriage) may be constricting, as Roland feared; it may also force a character to invent a way out. Ellen's musings on romance, and her willingness to play the role of baddie, show her to have been neither the kind of meek helpmeet eulogised by Beatrice Nest in her early book nor the sort of victim, alight with frustration and rage, expected by Leonora Stern and her band of Sapphist feminist critics. She's an example of how, set against the fixed archetypal backdrops of romance, the novel's characters come richly alive. To put it another way: the conventions of romance are evoked in order to facilitate character development, and a deeper sense of both comedy and pathos. Roland gains in moral stature by being small, sensitive and uncertain, not at all in control, not huge and heroic, armour-clad and sword-wielding. He has no need to search for the Grail, if by that is meant a symbol of men's lost femininity; as much as any female heroine of Mills & Boon he's allowed by his creator all the doubts, trembling and anxieties associated with that role. He wins through to sexual success, professional status and money (to stay within the terms of the genre) by being nimble-witted, like the heroes in Christabel's stories. He wins through because he can accept and share a woman's fantasy; he discovers that both he and Maud dream of autonomy, of sleeping alone in white beds in white rooms. Finally, of course, they share such a bed, at which point the novel, as a good romance should, moves towards its close. Roland has fought and conquered his dragon, and gets his reward: the Princess smiles upon him. (Maud is called the Princess by her friend Leonora; Christabel is given the same nickname by her friend Blanche.) Maud is both the dragon of feminism that he conquers – by being unalarming, gentle, respectful – and the heroine whose cold white beauty both attracts and repels. Maud's surname is Bailey: castle keeps that must be attacked, castle *baileys* that must be won, a fortress that must be taken:

> very slowly and with infinite gentle delays and delicate diversions and variations of indirect assault Roland finally, to use an outdated phrase, entered and took possession of all her white coolness that grew warm against him, so that there seemed to be no boundaries, and he heard, towards dawn, from a long way off, her clear voice crying out, uninhibited, unashamed, in pleasure and triumph.

Unlike Roland, Randolph Ash, the novel's nineteenth-century hero, has, a comfortable bourgeois home, a bit of power, a bit of prestige. But like Roland, though for different reasons, he's not the likeliest of heroes: he's no longer young, and he's heavily married. In him, the archetype of romance is not so much exploited, transgressed and transcended, as simply discovered. His first letter to Christabel, chanced upon, eagerly read, and then stolen, by Roland, is in fact a series of stuttering drafts, desperate attempts to find words, a trace of words lost then invented. Nothing could be more convincing than that falling in love means a poet, excited *by* speech, spurred *to* it, is then bereft *of* it, as Ash manages, at his second attempt, to tell Christabel in what he calls his 'egotistical mutter':

> *Did you not find it as strange as I did, that we should so immediately understand each other so well? For we did understand each other uncommonly well, did we not? Or is this perhaps a product of the over-excited brain of a middle-aged and somewhat disparaged poet, when he finds that his*

> *ignored, his arcane, his deviously perspicuous meanings, which he thought* not *meanings, since no one appeared able to understand them, had after all one clear-eyed and amused reader and judge?*

Ash woos Christabel with words: with conversation, with letters, with poems, with sensitive readings of her own poems. Like Roland, he demonstrates that to win a woman can entail being patient as well as eager, passive and accepting as well as active and outgoing, playful and childish as well as powerful and grown-up. (I'm suddenly reminded of Ladislaw in *Middlemarch* – how women readers have often understood why Dorothea liked him, while male critics have so often found him impossible). A man you can talk to, who'll listen, who'll also give of himself and talk back: this is more than a neat metaphor for good sex; it's the prelude to it; a necessity. Maud and Christabel respond to lovers who, in that old-fashioned phrase, treat them as persons, who see them not just as desiring but as speaking subjects; they are wary of importunate and devouring suitors (Fergus *Wolff*); of silencing and repressive ones. (Leonora talks too much, Blanche is too jealous and destroys Ash's letters – she wishes for 'mountain *ash* berries' to frighten away the 'Fairy Folk', the 'prowler' against whom Dog Tray's hackles go up like those of a '*wolf*' – wonderful projection here! She names Ash a Peeping Tom, but of course Christabel is learning she *likes* being looked at, being read, being known.)

I've been talking as though *Possession*, as a romance, tested itself only against the medieval versions of the genre, or the Victorian versions of the Arthurian. It does also, I think, make jokes about and play with more modern works and their pastiches of early nineteenth-century Gothic, of Jane Austen, of Shakespearian comedy. The ending of *Possession*, with its ludic sorting out of mismatched lovers into newly harmonious pairs, surely alludes to the end of Georgette Heyer's *The Grand Sophy* and its borrowings from *Midsummer Night's Dream* and *All's Well That Ends Well*, in which gags about the unsuitability of poets as spouses abound, and the three pairs of lovers' emotional turbulence is backed by suitably stormy weather, if not by the wonderfully Gothic coffin-opening sequence of *Possession.* Similarly, Christabel's decision to live in semi-retirement, in order to write, accompanied by her friend Blanche Glover, parallels the choice of Phoebe, the heroine of Georgette Heyer's who spurns the respectable, nay brilliant match offered by the saturnine Duke of Sale and who flees from him to try to set up house with her old governess and write novels. The novel of course rescues her from this spinsterly end: in the end she does fall in love with Sale and agree to marry him and we hear no more of governess friends or of novel-writing.

Ann Rosalind Jones, in the essay I quoted from earlier, suggests that the heroine of romance's apparent autonomy and freedom from family ties may mask her vulnerability and give the hero extra power over her: 'The heroine . . . is set in a social limbo: her family is dead or invisible, her friends are few or none, her occupational milieu is only vaguely filled in. As a result, her meeting with the hero occurs in a private realm which excludes all concerns but their mutual attraction; the rest of the world drops away except as a backdrop . . .'

To some extent *Possession* follows this formula. Both Christabel and Maud appear to have no close family that matters, though another branch of Maud's family, another lot of Baileys, provides the occasion for Maud and Roland to discover the hidden Ash–LaMotte letters (Baileys as *keepers* again), and though Christabel's married sister provides the means for hiding the daughter she bears as a result of her love affair with Ash: families as hiding places, as sites of repression.

What about Jones's claim that the heroine's friends are 'few or none'? Both heroines of *Possession* make a friend of their male lovers; as we've seen, that's the condition *sine qua non* which allows the courtship to proceed, become consummated. But what about their women friends, the confidantes and sparring partners so many of us outside the world of the romance find necessary? Certainly they don't exist in the world of Georgette Heyer, in the world of Mills & Boon, where women's needs for each other are firmly repressed and redirected solely towards men and heterosexual love, the mutual orgasm of the kiss that precedes marriage and closure. These romances, however witty and subversive in some ways, enact the myth that Freud claimed was universal: the need for the daughter to leave her mother, the world of women, and grow up, i.e. attach herself to a husband and find happiness in marriage. Freud recognised that the progress towards femininity wasn't easy, and the pleasure of romances comes partly from how they dramatise this anxiety and overcome it. Since our culture traditionally wishes girls to grow up into heterosexual wives and mothers, women's reading of romance is sanctioned at the same time that it is often despised. *Other* pleasures that women derive from reading romances, such as I mentioned above, are less rarely talked of, I believe because they are illicit – they raise the spectre of one woman getting pleasure from another.

It's this spectre, I believe, that *Possession* raises, only in the end to triumph over it. Blanche loves Christabel, but must give way to the superior claims of Randolph Ash. Leonora loves Maud, but must give way to Roland. For the myth of heterosexual romance to work satisfactorily, something must be given up. Not the hero but the heroine must renounce the love of the mother, in its physical and possessing aspect, and the love of other women where that touches upon lesbian drives.

Leonora, in contrast to Maud's fastidiously shrinking and

tightly wrapped virginal whiteness, is presented as exuberantly physical: she's big, with unbound breasts, she is for example:

> resplendent and barbaric in a scarlet silk shirt and trousers, faintly Oriental, faintly Peruvian, with woven rainbow-coloured borders. Her black hair flowed on her shoulders, her wrists and ears and visible bosom were hung with suns and stars of gold. She shone in the small space by the water-cooler and emitted pulses of florid and musky scent.

She messes up Maud's spotless green glass bathroom, littering it with puddles of water, lidless bottles and 'different spicy smells of unknown unguents . . . Opium or Poison'. She has a bisexual history and a stream of women lovers. She writes about Christabel as a Victorian lesbian and is exhaustingly voluble, yes a many-mouthed monster, kin to the medusas and melusinas who swim through the text and lure the unwary down to drown in their depths. Her sensuality is presented as suffocating, as maternal, as maternally suffocating:

> Leonora appeared in the doorway, largely naked except for an exiguous and unbelted crimson silk dressing-gown.
>
> 'A good-night kiss,' Leonora said.
>
> 'I can't.'
>
> 'You can. It's easy.'
>
> Leonora came to the bed and folded Maud into her bosom. Maud fought to get her nose free. Loose hands met Leonora's majestic belly and heavy breasts. She couldn't *push*, that was as bad as submitting. To her shame, she began to cry.
>
> 'What is it with you, Maud?'

I told you. I'm off the whole thing. Right off. I did tell you.'

'I can relax you.'

'*You must be able to see you have exactly the opposite effect.* Go back to bed, Leonora. Please.'

Leonora made various rrr-ooof noises like a large dog or bear, and finally rolled away, laughing. 'Tomorrow is another day,' said Leonora. 'Sweet dreams, Princess.'

Maud, that Tennysonian heroine, 'icily regular, splendidly null', sees Leonora as likeable but stifling. I, the reader, saw her as grotesque but comic: at least, I thought, she will survive, even though she has to be pushed to the margins of the romance. And she does: she's got her professorship, fresh work to do on LaMotte, her lover Mary-Lou, her ineradicable zest for life, sex and language. Leonora, I concluded, was just too Large to be confined in one of those clean white beds so beloved of Roland and Maud. She represents the wilder excesses of feminist scholarship that pushes soberly realist novelists to consider the constraints of what the Leonoras of this world argue are patriarchal forms and uses of language; she represents the edge of the feminist movement that insists that women must always put women first and that nothing is more natural than our desire to bond with each other politically and sexually. She is an offence to common sense. She is anarchic and free, which is why we're directed to laugh at her; she's a potential threat. She's drawn with affection as well as with satire, though she's not allowed the consummation of her desire for Maud.

Leonora comes across as full, as real. Not so Blanche Glover. Living her chosen hermit-like life with her beloved Christabel, she desires, we learn, to remain unseen: she avoids the gaze of others to concentrate on her work as an artist, as painter and illustrator.

Most of her work remains unseen, also unsold; she fails to make a living as an artist; her ambitions are too lofty, her canvases too large. We catch only glimpses of Blanche; briefly she swims into view in her short Journal which ends after she's written 'She was agitated; there were a few tears. We were quiet together, in our special ways, for a long time' and then that 'the Wolf is gone from the door'. Roland reads this Journal sitting in the Women's Archive at Lincoln University: 'a high-walled fish-tank' inside the main library, which is a 'glass box, with brilliant doors opening in glass . . . repeating panes, like Tinkerbell's fairylights in Never-Never-Land'. By the end of the novel we know that this evoking of fairyland and of the underwater kingdom of Is is ominous: Blanche, abandoned by Christabel, drowns herself, weighting her clothes with the big round stones brought back by Christabel from her secret trip to the north with Randolph Ash.

As her writings surface in the Women's Archive, so Blanche surfaces in the novel as scattered metaphors; she bobs on the text, dispersed as bits, phrases, odd words. She floats and won't sink; her presence haunts the romance. She is precisely an image of the return of the repressed. Throughout *Possession* there's a rich play on her name. Just as a glove bears the trace of the hand that it's moulded to cover, the hand that has withdrawn from it, Blanche Glover likes to trace – outlines, sketches – but is connected far more to absence than to fullness. The traces of herself she leaves behind seem negative. An inferior artist, she traces what Christabel calls 'our circumscribed little independence', or 'gold cage'. I think she may be the Black Artist, the jailer of the heroine in Christabel's story 'The Glass Coffin' – Black Artist, Blanche Artist, Blanche Glover, Blanche Lover – she wants to imprison Christabel, possess her, body and soul and text, just as the black attendants at the British Museum are described as warders and prison guards, jailing the Ash archive in the sulphurous Stygian gloom of the basement bookstacks. Blanche is an example of possession turned to possessiveness: she rejects, finally, the black jet friendship brooch given to her by Christabel; later, a hundred years later, when the book/body in the glass coffin has been opened/kissed back into life by Roland, Maud will offer the brooch to Leonora, in case Leonora may tackle better the quest for how to be a good female friend. It's not a quest central to the novel; and I think Leonora fails it. Blanche Glover's lack, her emptiness, her absence, are paradoxically summed up in Christabel's poem on gloves, a brilliant pastiche of Emily Dickinson –

Gloves lie together
Limp and calm
Finger to finger
Palm to palm
With whitest tissue
To embalm

In these quiet cases
White hands creep
With supple stretchings
Out of sleep
Fingers clasp fingers
Troth to keep

and perhaps a critique of what lesbians in the current women's movement dismiss as 'vanilla sex'. *Glover* contains a *lover* as Randolph Ash knows all too well; he wants to replace Blanche with himself; he writes to Christabel: 'I shall feel my way into your thought – as a hand into a glove – to steal your own metaphor and torture it cruelly – '. Finally, Blanche is written off by Sabine de Kercoz, written out, connected to suffocation and to masochism as the ultimate feminine heroine Elaine *Blanche Mains* (white hands) who is powerless against the prowler, the male wolf Ash:

> So the peasants and farmers, to make quite sure of their young ones, would close them inside the box-beds and make the door fast before going out to the fields,

Sabine writes:

> Wolves come; and there are men as bad as wolves; and there are sorcerers who believe they control such powers, and there is the peasant's faith in wolves and in the need to put solid doors between the child and all these dangers. In my childhood the fear of the wolves was hardly greater than the fear of being closed in, out of the light, into that box which resembled, at times a chest or shelf in a family vault as much as a safe retreat (a hermit's cave when I played at being Sir Lancelot, before I learned I was only a woman and must content myself with being Elaine aux Mains Blanches, who did nothing but suffer and complain and die).

Poor Blanche!

At the end of the traditional romance, the heroine disappears: into marriage, into the marital bedroom. That's where we lose sight of Maud, in the bed she consents at last to share with Roland. Tenderly, firmly, the door is shut upon them and our voyeuristic pleasure brought to an end, though not before we have discovered that Maud is in fact descended from both Christabel and Randolph Ash, that Christabel's fading from view, her dwindling into silence and obscurity, is compensated for by the daughter she bears and by the handing on of the gift of poetry to future generations.

I'll end where I began, with Roland in the garden. With paradise regained after the Fall. With the bursting up inside him of poetry. For it's here that the novel's climax happens, I think, not in those cool white beds, and it's a climax linked to what those French feminists, beloved I am sure of Leonora Stern, call *la jouissance*: the utterance of poetic language as a feminine pleasure recalling the baby's blissful babble at the maternal breast; poetry as anti-logical and anti-patriarchal, poetry as the language that lets men discover their femininity and let go of the clichés associated with the Law of the Father. *Jouissance*, or pleasure, becomes linked in *Possession* to the acts both of reading and of writing. In this brilliant postmodern romance it's the reader who's the true lover, the truest lover: all the main characters in the novel, poets, scholars, diarists, autobiographers, biographers, secretaries and lawyers, are set on fire by what they read. They read and chase each other's texts in a glorious literary orgy; texts circulate, come together, pastiche themselves into other texts, transcend censorship, theft, suppression, fire, burial and decay. Roland, who began by being a passionate reader, will now become a passionate writer, a purveyor of *jouissance* to others. I've suggested that *Possession*, as a romance celebrating heterosexual love, has to repress the words for love between women. Nevertheless, throughout the novel, they rise, and rise again, and the pleasure they indicate surfaces – atavistic, polymorphous perverse – in the response of the reader to this dazzling, satisfying text, which is warm, fulfilling and generous as that lost paradise we dream of, that lost maternal body made to live again in writing: 'it was always there . . . we . . . knew it was always there, and have always known it was as it was, though we have now for the first time recognised, become fully cognisant of, our knowledge'.

Possession restores us to what we have lost: to fullness, to completion, to closure, in order to evoke a new beginning. The novel opens with a quotation from Ash's *The Garden of Proserpina* –

These things are there. The garden and the tree
The serpent at its root, the fruit of gold
The woman in the shadow of the boughs
The running water and the grassy space.

– and reaches its end (one of its several endings, I should say) when Roland, in the garden, muses on the words 'golden' and 'apples' and feels poetry begin inside him. The ancient myth of love between women, of a mother's passionate love for her daughter, with all the ambivalence, the toing and froing, the separating and the reuniting, which that love entails, is made to come to life in the poetry of one man, Ash, and handed on to another, Roland. Roland, the gentle knight, the friendly tamer of dragons, has found a kind of Holy Grail after all. He carries it inside him. He is a container and maker and re-maker of words. What he will do with those lists of words he's made, that 'golden' those 'apples', is the matter for another romance.

ON FAIRY TALES AND THEIR TELLERS: *FROM THE BEAST TO THE BLONDE*

by Marina Warner

Independent on Sunday, 14 October 1994

Marina Warner is one of the great synthesizers and bridge-builders. As much as she deconstructs the myths of Western culture (the Virgin Mary, Joan of Arc the female warrior, the ambiguities of allegory and virtue posed as female) she reassembles them so that we can not only see how they're made but enjoy their lasting power and attraction. She steps from scholarship to popular culture and back again. She brings the fruits of scholarly labours, her own and others', to a wide modern audience. She bestows these gifts of understanding and insight with tremendous enthusiasm. Her arguments are never cold and dry, but persuasive, cajoling, even seductive. She writes so beautifully that I am sure even her VAT returns are a joy to behold. Just like the tale-tellers she celebrates in this mammoth study, she's an elegant word-spinner, a weaver of enchantments, each sentence a silken knot charming you further into her web of meanings which she ravels and unravels with dizzying speed and skill. For the sheer pleasure of its prose alone this book is hard to beat.

Angela Carter is its presiding fairy godmother, hovering over it as though in blessing. She appears on the opening pages, invoked as an exemplary, witty anthologist of fairy tales who can offer others nourishing and delicious 'meat of the tongue', and she pops up in the closing paragraphs to stress the collective nature of the genre's creation: 'Ours is a highly individualised culture, with a great faith in the work of art as a unique one-off, and the artist as an original, a godlike and inspired creator of unique one-offs. But fairy tales are not like that, and nor are their makers. Who first invented meatballs? In what country? Is there a definitive recipe for potato soup? Think in terms of the domestic arts. "This is how I make potato soup."'

The appeal for Warner is, she happily admits, a personal one. Fairy tales 'seemed to offer the possibility of change, far beyond the boundaries of their improbable plots or fantastically illustrated pages . . . like romance, to which fairy tales bear a strong affinity, they could "remake the world in the image of desire". That this is a blissful dream which need not be dismissed as totally foolish is central to the argument of this book.'

This argument is a historical one: that if we wish to understand fairy tales then far from eliciting some transcendent timeless essence they supposedly possess we need to investigate first of all 'the context in which they were told . . . who was telling them, to whom, and why'. Furthermore, 'the thrust towards universal significance has obscured the genre's equal powers to illuminate experiences embedded in social and material conditions. These are subject to change over time and ultimately more capable of redress than the universal lessons of greed, lust and cruelty which fairy tales give us; in one sense, the historical interpretation of fairy tales holds out more hope to the listener or the reader than the psychoanalytical or mystical approaches, because it reveals how human behaviour is embedded in material circumstance, in the laws of dowry, land tenure, feudal obedience, domestic hierarchies and marital dispositions, and that when these pass and change, behaviour may change with them.' As someone who in the past has relished Jungian interpretations of fairy tales by analysts such as Marie-Louise von Franz and Nor Hall, I find this new route into reading original and helpful. It certainly makes you take a second and third look at Cinderella, Snow White, Sleeping Beauty, and the rest of that girls' gang, at just *what* the perils were that they were negotiating.

But before we get on to the cake of Bluebeard and Donkeyskin's incestuous dad and all those evil stepmothers in Part Two, first of all we must eat our bread and butter in Part One. Very rich and filling it is too, in fact far from a nursery tea unfit for sophisticated tastes. From the start Warner reassures us that though fairy tales may appear to evoke childish matters for childish audiences they are extremely artful and complicated in both content and telling: 'there is nothing in the least childlike about fairy tales, and this, together with the suspect whiff of femininity hanging around them, attracted me to study them'.

That 'suspect whiff' sounds as though it might be quite sexy, and indeed turns out to be so. Female sexuality was a pivot around which whirled contemporary fantasies of the storytellers themselves and the urgently expressed power-politics content of their tales. Of course women were not the only traditional tellers of fairy tales, but Warner makes a convincing case for the way in which the figure of the narrator being read as female allowed for the expression of all sorts of feminine concerns and obsessions. Female experience, female dreads and desires, form the core, and sex is the pip in the apple: good sex and dreary sex, marital sex and illicit sex. It comes dressed up in a myriad disguises, as we already know from our dreams: 'elements of Greek romance, Roman moralities, Arabian nights, animal fables, medieval jests, pious saints' lives jostle and unite with unbuttoned lack of inhibition. The nature of the genre is promiscuous and omnivorous and anarchically heterogeneous, absorbing high and low elements, tragic and comic tones into its often simple, rondo-like structure of narrative.'

The narrators who could handle all these demands on their technique ignored an ancient injunction laid on women: hold your tongue! Women's speech, imaged by anxious patriarchs as licentious and anti-authority, had to be controlled just like women's sexuality did too; one pair of lips opening and closing mirrored another pair, lower down. So Warner argues that fairy tales, intimately connected to women talking, are part of a complex web of relationships of taboos, myths and jokes around the idea, let alone the practice, of women creating art out of words. She whisks us into a storytellers' labyrinth, where we encounter sibyls, nurses, Fates, old wives, gorgons, *précieuses ridicules*, muses, Gammer Gurtons, Mother Geese, gossips, godmothers, midwives, storks, crones, witches, monsters, Saint Anne and the Queen of Sheba. In successive chapters we meet and get to know these figures, and then Warner, whom we have trusted all along as our Ariadne, reels in her connecting thread and winds us out again, ready to hear the tales themselves. Just occasionally, wandering along these archive corridors, I did get lost in the minutiae of detail, even though the succeeding paragraph made things clear again. Warner is such a generous writer. She pours her conclusions at the reader, eager to share not only her ideas but her process of discovery. Reading this book is like reading one of those medieval encyclopaedists for whom everything in the world is connected to everything else. Just listen to this characteristically passionate exposition on geese as emblematic creatures for gossips: 'In French, the verb *cacarder* is used for the noise made by a goose; *caquet* or chatter, as we saw, means women's talk as well as the goose's cry. Not as onomatopoeic as the English "honk", *cacarder* does catch the coprological side of infantile existence more than "cackle". However, the associations of the bird do not end there. Geese strike erotic not just scatological resonances; they were sacred to Isis as well as to Aphrodite, who uses them as her flying steeds, standing on an outstretched bird in a dish from Boetia of the sixth century BC, and riding most gracefully sidesaddle on a particularly beautiful white ground kylix made around 460 BC (though it must be said that it is not always possible, in the silence of monochrome artefacts, to tell geese and swans apart). The goose was specifically sacred to Peitho, the nymph who personifies Persuasion and stands at Aphrodite's side in scenes of seduction – the embodiment of her sweet-talking tongue. In France *la petite-oie*, little goose, was used of fripperies of dress, and, by extension, of favours begged and received by lovers.' The great benefit of all this richness of text is the way it demonstrates the source of Warner's theses. She is not a didactic writer; she teaches by demonstration.

In Part Two she looks at the stories themselves, probing all the old favourites to reveal the disturbing themes at their heart, the dilemmas posed for and by beauties and beasts, reluctant brides, runaway girls, silent fathers, anxious stepmothers, silent daughters. These chapters re-distil the powerful magic of what we can no longer call archetypes; Warner makes an elegant case for seeing these protagonists as deeply enmeshed in particular histories. For example, if women marry young, keep having children, and often die in childbed, then men marry and remarry and remarry, and so all the anxieties of Bluebeard's newest wife of necessity parade themselves in the bloody chamber, which is womb and marital bedroom and memory all at once, and which may link cradles to coffins in all too real a way. Nightmares are grounded in reality; fairy stories examine and attempt to dispel them. Crucial aspects of the tales, Warner suggests, circle the insecurity experienced by older women. For example in the Rapunzel story 'the old woman's desire for the baby girl corresponds to material needs for helping hands at home, and reflects the arranged transfer of girls to other families as prospective wives, or surrogate domestic servants. Her furious intervention between the girl and her suitor would then relate the conflicting, simultaneous fears of redundancy growing in a widowed woman whose son's marriage has made her insecure in what used to be her home, under her control. The vilification of older women in such interpretations belongs in a long tradition . . . Hatred of the older woman, and intergenerational strife, may arise not only from rivalry, but from guilt, too, about the weak and the dependent. The portrait of the tyrant mother-in-law or stepmother may conceal her own vulnerability, may offer an excuse for her maltreatment . . . A mother-in-law had good reason to fear her son's wife, when she often had to strive to maintain her position and assert her continuing rights to a livelihood in the patrilineal household.'

The heart of the book consists of Warner's lengthy, learned and infinitely tender dissection and defence of the secrets in families which give birth to fairy stories. She makes us look again at 'the stock villain, the wicked stepmother' who may not even be a stepmother at all but a wet-nurse or helper, while 'the evil she does is not intrinsic to her nature, or to the strict maternal relation, or to her particular family position. It cannot and should not be extended to all women, for it arises from the insecurity of her interests in a social and legal context that can be changed, and remedied . . . Nannies use bogeymen to frighten children into obedience, and a woman storyteller might well displace the harsher aspects of her command on to another woman, a rival who can take the blame. But this is a social stratagem, not an ineluctable or Oedipal condition, and mothers or stepmothers today need not be inculpated *en masse.* As remarriage becomes more and more common, stepmothers find they are tackling a hard crust of bigotry set in the minds of their new children, and refreshed by endless returns of the wicked stepmother in the literature of childhood.' Just so. In the same way, few of us today would wish to dub all fathers and step-fathers incestuous beasts and rapists, yet daughters running away from sexuality (their own and their fathers' when too painfully tangled together) will still find the Donkeyskin or Peau d'Ane stories helpful and consoling. I've indicated only a few of the riches of this marvellous book, which is for *all* of us; just as fairy tales are; revealing the healing powers of the imagination and showering us with its delights.

UNDER MY SKIN

by Doris Lessing

The Sunday Times, 3 October 1995

Few of the main protagonists of Doris Lessing's major novels have childhoods. Martha Quest, heroine of the *Children of Violence* series, arrives on page one as a brooding, rebellious adolescent. Anna, who dominates *The Golden Notebook*, is a young woman who's already published her first novel, whose flashbacks to an earlier self concern only her adult past. It's probably impossible to overestimate the profound impact these novels have had on generations of readers eager for their intellectual, political and moral challenge, but you did wonder, as you read them, *why* the stories apparently required these ardent characters to remember only part of their pasts. You wondered especially because you realised that the novels drew upon lived experience and transformed it, extending the personal into a wider realm, what Lessing herself calls 'the general', via omniscient narration. *Memoirs of a Survivor* was a fascinating book in this particular respect, for it unusually and memorably made childhood central to its drama: modern childhood, and also what seemed a Victorian childhood, a painful, disturbing one.

In this autobiography Lessing tells the story of her life in what was then Southern Rhodesia, up to her departure for England in 1949, and gives her childhood the space it deserves, in terms of children's experience of the passing of time: 'how far away it was, the condition of being grown-up and free, for I was still in the state where the end of the day could hardly be glimpsed from its start . . . there is no way of conveying in words the difference between child time and grown-up time . . . in the story of a life, if it is being told true to time as actually experienced, then I'd say seventy per cent of the book would take you to age ten. At eighty per cent you would have reached fifteen. At ninety-five per cent you get to about thirty. The rest is a rush – towards eternity.'

Lessing's memories begin in Persia, as it was called then. She brilliantly conveys the child's intensity of experiencing the world, in images that link with those in *Memoirs of a Survivor*: 'The Tehran nursery was English, Edwardian, and could have been in London . . . The air in that room is all smells. The scorch of newly ironed cloth, vaseline, Elliman's Embrocation, cod-live oil, almond oil, camphorated oil, Pears soap, the nostril-expanding tang from the copper jug and basin on the wash-stand, the airless smell of flames, paraffin from the little stove that heats bottles and milk, the smell of the contents of the two pots . . . Heavy curtains hold dust, behind them muslin curtains with their smell of soap, and the wood smells of furniture polish. The curtains have blue and pink Bo-peeps and lambs, but otherwise everything, but everything, is white. A suffocation of smelly whiteness.'

Persia gave the child images of sustenance – water flowing in stone irrigation channels, a kindly shepherd – but could not be other than a backdrop to scenes of child-rearing some of us have learned to call brutal and cruel when we see them being re-enacted today, or remember them from our own experience. The idea was that a child was a *thing*, a dirty little animal who had to learn who was boss, whose feeding and excreting had to be rigorously controlled, whose privacy and sense of self had to be constantly invaded in the name of teaching clean habits. The author of this regime was Dr Truby King, whose manual taught generations of mothers never to pick up crying babies, to feed them only at four-hourly intervals and to let them scream with hunger in between times, and to hold them over the pot from birth onwards.

Lessing relates these horrors with honesty and compassion, and with some ambivalence as well. On the one hand she lines up the deprivations of her early childhood with 'the emotional hurts which are common, are the human condition, part of everyone's infancy' and is understanding towards her mother: 'she was only doing what all good parents did . . . Now I see her as a tragic figure, living out her disappointing years with courage and with dignity.' On the other hand she records: 'as my mother cheerfully told me, again and again, I was starved for the first ten months of my life . . . Why did my mother need to tell her little daughter, so often, and with such enjoyment, that she had been starved by her mother all through her infancy? . . . What I remember is hard bundling hands, impatient arms and her voice telling me over and over again that she had not wanted a girl, she wanted a boy. I knew from the beginning she loved my brother unconditionally, and she did not love me.' While Lessing concludes that 'my early childhood made me one of the walking wounded for years', simultaneously she wonders why such an 'extraordinary degree of malice and vindictiveness goes into the combat' between mothers and adolescent daughters. Yet surely that's the rage of the helpless child surfacing when the time comes to separate. Reading this painful account, characterised by so puzzled a tenderness, made me realise *why* Martha Quest's mother was presented, in *Children of Violence*, as quite such a monster. The wounds go deep, and are ancient. Anger that isn't recognised festers for years. And because parents forget the well-intentioned cruelty they inflict upon their children, they can never apologise for it. The child has to cope with the damage and the burden of pain and rage on her own. In

Lessing's case this seems to have required that she abandon her two small children by her first husband, presumably in case she ended up damaging them in her turn. Though she doesn't put it like that: in her late twenties the passionate young woman used the language of politics, of building a better world. Interpreting these episodes, I've been using the language of Alice Miller, whose books on psychology are recent.

Lessing pictures herself, early on in this wonderful autobiography, watching her parents sitting outside their mud and thatch house in the Rhodesian bush, both of them irrevocably wounded by their losses and suffering in the First World War: 'There they are, together, *stuck together*, held there by poverty and – much worse – secret and inadmissible needs that come from deep in their two so different histories . . . I stand there, a fierce unforgiving adamant child, saying to myself: I won't. I will not. I will not be like that . . . *Don't be like them.* Meaning, never let yourself be trapped. In other words, I was rejecting the human condition, which is to be trapped by circumstances.' At the risk of sounding stupidly and offensively reductive, I need to say that this passage, and the others I've quoted, illuminate aspects of Lessing's writing I've found difficult: her occasional loftiness as a narrator, for example, her seeing omniscience, the wisdom that some of her characters use to transcend ordinary human muddle and mess. Here, she makes you see where that urge towards transcendence comes from.

What she makes us see, too, is how the girl's anger fuelled both the rebel and the writer, the search for facts with which to fight back. Passionate descriptions of the beauties of the bush and the space it afforded for escape and adventure become images for a changed world: 'I wandered about the bush or sat on an antheap, angry to the point of being crazy myself, seeing my parents as they were now and what they should have been – and from here it is only a step to the thought, If we make war impossible the world will be full of whole and healthy and sane and marvellous people who . . . In my mind I lived in utopias, part from literature and part the obverse of what I actually lived in.' The story of Lessing's flight to the city, of her growing awareness of the injustices perpetrated by the white minority coupled with her politicisation and membership of Communist groups, has been told by her in her series *Children of Violence*. In the autobiographical version she gives us here there are more details, more context and background, more anecdotes. She insists on the authenticity of the novels: it's a vision of realism as *truth* that has been out of fashion for a while and is beginning to be reappreciated. Her first novel, *The Grass Is Singing*, which she went on redrafting while surviving all kinds of losses and shocks, distils all that sharp observation she'd learned at a young age. The autobiography, riveting from beginning to end, closes just where the novels start, with the birth into freedom, adulthood, the blank pages of the next book.

WALKING IN THE SHADE

by Doris Lessing

Independent, 13 October 1997

There are marvellous treasures in this book. If Doris Lessing has been popularly imagined (or marketed) in recent years as the serene sibyl dispensing Sufistic wisdom from on high, then this second volume of her memoirs tweaks that image into place by throwing off the oracle's dark veil and revealing the frivolous layers underneath. Recently arrived in England from what was then Rhodesia, rejoicing in post-war efforts to abandon austerity and invent new kinds of sensual fun, she tells us how all right-thinking (which included left-thinking) young women made regular trips to Paris: 'There is no way now of telling how powerful a dream France was then . . . Now that our cooking and our coffee and our clothes are good, it is hard to remember how people yearned for France as for civilisation itself. And there was another emotion too, among women. French men loved women and showed it, but in Britain the most women could hope for was to be whistled at by workmen in the street, not always a friendly thing . . . When I went to Paris my toilette was hardly of the level to attract French compliments, but it was true every man gave you a quick, expert once-over – hair, face, what you were wearing – allotting you marks. This was a dispassionate, disinterested summing-up, not necessarily leading to invitations . . . Adorable France, which loves its women, gives them confidence in their femininity.' If you don't want to be gazed at and judged *all* the time, then it makes sense to nip over to Paris just occasionally, buy a hat as Lessing did, and then return to the invisibility which is the precondition for writing novels. This anecdote encapsulates one of the themes in Lessing's writings which she might want to call minor but which nonetheless has fascinated generations of her readers: all the contradictions women struggle with about love and friendship with men, wanting to be loved and appreciated, but on whose terms? The fifties version of the Real Woman, all nipped-in waists and simultaneous orgasms, vaginal not clitoral of course for the woman, dramatised all sorts of conflicts around fear and desire, dependence and independence, change and staying still. An intellectual who loved men, cherished their company and conversation, earned her own living and was a single mother to boot, was a rare creature in those days, the exception who proved the rule.

Somewhere else, in Paris, were those women-loving men not frightened of women with brains? Yet sooner or later even they might have started demanding lunch on the table at one o'clock sharp and leaving her to mind the baby alone. One of the strongest threads in this long and sometimes rambling account of the fifties concerns what's now called the sex war but which in those days could be characterised as a quest: Childe Doris to the Dark Tower came. She quickly discovered that men who praised your frocks did not necessarily stick around after drinks and bed to discuss your soul. Let alone your novels. Luckily, she found a good agent, Juliet O'Hea, who sold her first novel, *The Grass Is Singing*, to Michael Joseph, and gave her emotional support and good advice. Lessing is delightful on the mean ways of publishers who only publicise bestsellers and neglect their mid-list. But Michael Joseph was a sweetie who took her to lunch at the Caprice, all pink tablecloths and glittering silver, and talked charmingly of Larry and Viv. He admired her cool about sales figures whereas she didn't realise that all these rushes into reprinting were astonishing.

Anyway, in Paris Lessing stayed in the shabby hotel where Oscar Wilde had died, in the very room. She does not report whether the infamous wallpaper was still in place (Wilde said of this wallpaper 'either it goes or I do' and then expired) but she sketches a picture of *la patronne* voluptuous and radiant as anything in Degas: 'It was a dark, cluttered room, with mirrors gleaming from corners, shawls over chairs, a cat. There was Madame, in an armchair, flesh bulging over her pink corset, her fat feet in a basin of water. The maid, a young girl, was brushing her rusty old hair, while Madame tossed it back as if it were a treasure.'

Why should that be so? Well, Lessing wrote out of a passionate need to tell the truth, a conviction that realism could do the job. Although she was depicting scenes never before considered by English audiences, the horrors of the apartheid system and the brutal depersonalising of the oppressed, she emulated her great nineteenth-century English forebears who established realism of different sorts as adequate to explore their culture. Sometimes, in her mocking interjections, she can sound like Trollope or Thackeray. Sometimes she teeters towards caricature and pantomime like Dickens. Sometimes she is a wise owl like George Eliot, slipping in moral asides. What she's not, in most of her fiction, is a modernist. She delights in reporting the wily ins and outs of conversations as Henry James did, but, unlike James whose meandering sentences built a bridge towards the streams of unconscious thought explored by Virginia Woolf and Dorothy Richardson and James Joyce, she settles with her omniscient narrators who know what's going on in every mind and can tell us so in plain prose. Perhaps that style of writing went with her socialism, which was the sort insisting that the vanguard knew what was best for everybody else. Even though, in the early Martha Quest books, we ostensibly view the world of wartime left-wing politics in southern Africa refracted through the mind of a particular young woman, we're often made aware, as the critic Nicole Ward Jouve has pointed out, that Lessing the omniscient narrator keeps breaking in.

Perhaps the consciousness of one young woman just isn't adequate for understanding twentieth-century politics? Certainly Lessing was a pioneer in exploring whether that were so. If she felt that she had to jump in and bolster it up from a more supposedly objective point of view then that just shows the difficulty of the project. But you do notice, reading the early novels, how they seem to be written some of the time from a superego which eschews humour in favour of scorn, an emotion Lessing admits came easily to her at that time. Indeed, there doesn't seem to have been much to make jokes about, if you were not a satirist like Muriel Spark, say, or lighting a particular torch like Angus Wilson. Lessing was writing about the failures and betrayals of the Stalinist attempt at socialism, and very bleak it sounds too. Those of us who were on the left in those days, or a little later on, in the sixties, in the leftish branch of the women's movement, can remember and sympathise with the difficulties of being an artist at that time, when to want just to make things was seen as bourgeois self-indulgence, and when telling the truth meant dealing with disinformation and paranoia. In this volume of the autobiography Lessing gets all that off her chest in sections which are perhaps a little too long and could have been edited down a bit. You do feel their raw pain.

Her personal account does however add a fascinating series of footnotes to the novels. Though feminism arrived just too late, in its newest wave, to be of use to her, just an irritating blip at the edge of her screen obscuring her world view, *The Golden Notebook* has been consistently read as a woman's book. In this most experimental of her novels, Lessing exploded integrated form and consistent narrative viewpoint to demonstrate that post-war women were flying apart, falling apart – bombs, orgasms, breakdowns – and that men, as well as politics, were crucially involved. Here, in the memoir, she names names, and what a pleasure we get from hearing them. This novel made her a foremother to those of us coming after her, for in it she investigated whether the artist was sexless or androgynous, whether a woman artist had to keep her femininity apart from her writing and wear it in her life like a sort of disguise while in her work she could be big and tough, whether you *could* perfect both the life and the work. Me, I love the Lessing who appreciated that Colettish landlady in her seedy backroom, her shameless and knowledgeable body.

INCIDENTS IN THE RUE LAUGIER

by Anita Brookner

and

BEHIND CLOSED DOORS

by Alina Reyes

The Sunday Times, 3 June 1994

Would it be just a tease, a come-on, to claim that, contrary to what you might expect, these two novels are in many ways alike? It must be admitted that their authors, up until now, have been perceived as being as different as chalk and Camembert. Alina Reyes' literary reputation rests on her capacity for steamy raunchiness, for writing about sex as graphically as any man. We're supposed to be amazed that a woman can write such posh bodice-rippers, can produce such poetic paeans to the penis, despite the fact that Anaïs Nin was doing it forty years ago. *Plus ça change* . . . Anita Brookner, on the other hand, the doyenne of the slowly unbuttoned cardigan, tends to be praised for her Jamesian subtlety and reticence. Alina Reyes's wistful heroines are always slipping off their silk knickers and coming at the drop of a zip, whereas Anita Brookner's more discreet ladies rarely mention their underwear or their orgasms at all. Reyes knows that sex sells, that the frantically curious child in each of us still wants to peep through the keyhole of the parents' bedroom, that some of us can be titillated by reading about sex separated from emotion, 'pure' sex in a context free of memory or thought. Anita Brookner, by contrast, has concentrated on feeling to the exclusion of sex, keeps that bedroom door firmly locked, those curtains tightly drawn, reveals not so much naked flesh as a deep ambivalence about modern women's appetites for pleasure and power. She writes most perceptively about the mighty heroism both expressed and concealed by small acts of good manners.

How interesting, then, to find Brookner's latest novel exploring sexual obsession and desire, while Reyes', for all its apparent permissiveness, ends up celebrating finding your true love and riding off into the sunset.

Both books toy with the modernist notion that a work of art must demonstrate subject as form, must show how it's made. Brookner begins in the first person, announcing on page two: 'please accept me as an unreliable narrator . . . When I was clearing my mother's flat . . . I found a notebook from which I have constructed the story which follows.' From the inspiration of a few scribbled French words springs the novel that follows, written in the most conventional and traditional way from the perspective of an omniscient narrator. It's hard to believe that the first, brief, chapter really matters at all. Reyes gives us the novel as *soixante-neuf*, its two halves, printed top to tail, purporting to offer the point of view of both genders. This playful device obscures the novel's lack of plot and character. The fact that at the end of each chapter the reader is given the 'choice' of which chapter to read next means little, since these episodes don't advance a story but repeat sexual encounters, in the best tradition of pornography, piling one on top of the other *ad infinitum*, providing a hall of mirrors which yawns into the distance. Heavy breathing is soon overtaken by sighs of boredom.

Both books deal with holiday romance, and both evoke French landscapes of a vanished or invisible sort. Brookner tells a bittersweet tale straight out of one of her beloved nineteenth-century French authors, as mournful as Balzac's *Eugénie Grandet*, with its account of virginal love betrayed, as tragic as Maupassant's *Vie d'une femme*, with its hearty relish of youthful mistakes leading to adult disaster. Her heroine Maud, seeking to escape her dull, conventional life in Dijon in the late sixties, the safe advantageous marriage planned for her by her mother, falls for Tyler, the most charming of cads, the most rotten of bounders, the sort we've all bedded and loved at some point in our *éducation sentimentale*. This being pre-Pill France, however, another metaphor for Brookner country, the passive helpless Maud, once abandoned by her Don Juan of a seducer, needs rescuing. Enter Tyler's friend Harrison, who falls in love with Maud, marries her, takes her back to England to the sort of respectable and comfortable existence she fled from, and spends the rest of his life increasingly consumed by anguish that she doesn't love or desire him. Harrison is given all the moral grandeur of those nineteenth-century heroines, all the yearning inarticulate desires conventionally associated with femininity. His is an intriguing character when seen from the inside. Most of the time, Brookner's prose keeps us detached, at a distance. Only her rooms are full of life, express their owners' feelings. Though her subject is sexual desire and its consequences, she is reticent about the acts involved. Here is Maud's first encounter with Tyler: 'Then he turned her round, put his hands on her waist, and laid her down gently on to the bare boards. "I have never done this before" she said. "I knew" he replied. "That's all right."'

No such inhibitions for Reyes. Not only does she call a spade a penis, but, in the best male sporting tradition, can transform a penis into a dart. Or a sword, or a dagger, or an *épée*. Her little *jeu d'espirit* takes us into a fairground booth, and thence through lots of different doors into different sorts of sexual spectacles and games. She leaves no buttocks unturned, no orifice unfilled. Pints of semen spill through her pages in the most generous way: 'At the fourth thrust of his *épée*, he stretched out between my breasts and splashed me in abundance, up to my chin. Enticed by the fragrance of his unguent I began to tongue the tip of his now flaccid dart, and then I took it in my mouth and gave him such bounty that once more, between my lips, it began to become inflamed. He yelled out loud when I extracted the last of his sap, which I swallowed with relish.' That these pastiches of courtly love tales come across as comic is probably not the translator's fault: 'I reached out my hand and grabbed that thick, warm love cone that swelled beneath his britches . . . Pulling at his britches I discovered a proud dart and two fair-haired balls which fanned my rage . . . with one push, he fucked me. We quickly came together.' And so on and on and on.

Both novels circle obsessively around the notion of the male lover as a god and his penis as an emblem of his divinity. Poor penis, having to carry such enormous symbolic weight. If these weren't romances, you'd expect some buckling under the strain. The wise Maud, in Brookner's tale, takes to her *chaise-longue* and reads Colette. I'd advise following her example.

ANAÏS NIN

by Deirdre Bair

The Sunday Times, 3 June 1995

Anaïs Nin's posthumous fame rests on the publication of her voluminous diaries and their supposedly frank admissions of unbridled sexuality, on her astonishing capacity for lying to all her intimates, on the pornography she wrote to raise money for her lover Henry Miller, and on her image as the ultra-feminine Bohemian, the child-woman so dear to the surrealist imagination, the Painted Lady whose wings were of steel. By the time of her death, in the mid-seventies, she was hailed by some as a feminist icon, as an archetype of the unashamedly free woman, the patron saint of confessional writing who had become mother and muse to a coterie of devoted acolytes. To others she was a monster of narcissism, deceit and vanity, whose desperate and bizarre behaviour verged on the pathological, who was greedy, spoilt, manipulative and ruthless.

A reputation spanning such contradictory extremes is common to many twentieth-century women artists struggling to discover whether the codes of conventional feminine behaviour encourage or suppress talent, but in Nin's case it indicates also the depths of turbulence inside her which she was never able totally to control. If her effect on others was to provoke ecstatic admiration one moment and bitchy hostility the next, perhaps this had something to do with her inability to see herself as ordinary. Her credo was 'living the dream', which in her case originated in her need to overcome the nightmare experiences of her childhood. From being an actor in her father's myth of omnipotence, she grew into someone obsessed by myths, a writer who created them and tried to live them out, who was to some extent trapped by them. Rather than study Nin's story as fairy tale or myth, however, Deirdre Bair has chosen to give us a conventional, lengthy, blow by blow account of the 'real facts' of Nin's life, painstakingly researched, indexed and annotated, thereby conferring on Nin the status of what she calls: 'a major minor writer'.

One most important fact that must have definitively shaped Anaïs Nin's adult personality was her father's sexual abuse of her as a child. Deirdre Bair mentions this almost simply in passing, but it seems key to understanding Nin's later behaviour. Her Catalan father Joaquin, a talented musician, was unstable and cruel. He would lock his three children in their bedrooms while he beat their mother, Rosa. Next, he took to locking up Rosa first, then beating the children, so that her screams punctuated their cries. He liked to make the children march up to the dark and frightening attic, hitting them, as they mounted the stairs, with a hairbrush, a cane, or the flat of his hand. He would lock the children inside the attic, beating the boys first, then sending them away while he turned his attention to Anaïs. At the age of seventeen, after her father's desertion of his family, Anaïs wrote: 'I would do anything to keep him from lifting my dress and beating me.'

She wrote about these incidents many times in her diary throughout her life, recording how her father constantly taunted her with being ugly, while at the same time clearly being obsessed with her. It is notoriously difficult to retain accurate memories of this sort of trauma, since we protect ourselves from terrible pain by trying to forget and deny it, but Nin concluded, years later: 'I do not believe my father penetrated me sexually but I believe he caressed me while or instead of beating me.' When she was eleven, her father stopped beating her, but found a new method of punishment and humiliation. He began to photograph the children when they were in the bath, bursting in on them and forcing them to stand and face the camera. Besides photographing Anaïs naked in the bath, he followed her with the camera as she dressed in the morning and undressed at night, all the while repeating the refrain: 'what an ugly little girl'. Nin's diary-writing, obsessive as any neurosis, is surely her attempt to create a compensatory parallel world in which by having power over words, she could imagine having power over people. Similarly, the way in which she compulsively rewrote the diary, altering and refining her versions of events, suggests her attempts to integrate these traumatic and destabilising experiences, to forge them into something she could live with, bear to acknowledge. It was hard for her to admit what really happened, because she felt so guilty at having experienced sexual arousal along with the pain. Her lying, later in life, re-enacts that inability to tell 'what really happened', just as her masochistic giving of her self, her time and her money to many worthless male lovers acts out her confusion and her shame. She was desperate for male approval of her beauty and talent, and who can blame her after that inauspicious start. Similarly, she seems to have believed she must make herself sexually available to all the men she met; that was what her father taught her, after all.

Damaged people are often unpleasant. They are too busy designing survival strategies to be nice. Anaïs Nin does not sound at all nice. But you end up admiring her sheer cussed determination to stick her foot in the door and enter the world on her own terms. Unfortunately, this involved controlling and manipulating her husband, the one man in her life who did indeed adore her and offer her the security she craved. She married the wealthy

Hugo Guiler after her peripatetic European childhood was completed by an education in America. Hugo, born in Boston and brought up in Puerto Rico, he appreciated Anaïs' mix of Spanish and Cuban inheritance. Their honeymoon in Havana was soon followed by a move to Paris. Hugo, the hardworking banker, provided the money that allowed Anaïs to furnish the flat of her fantasies with Gothic shutters, Moroccan furniture, copper tables and a balcony sleeping loft. It was 1925. Anaïs defied fashion by refusing to drink cocktails. She toyed with flamenco dancing, went on with the diary, and spent her housekeeping money on a troop of lovers that included Henry Miller and her analyst Dr René Allendy. Bair's accounts of Nin darting between assignations, desperately trying to keep all her affairs afloat, are as sad as they are funny.

After the outbreak of war, when Anaïs and Hugo fled to the States, tragi-comedy became pure farce, as Anaïs, all the while slowly building her literary career, became a bigamist, wedding Rupert Pole, with whom she lived in California, while remaining married to Hugo, whom she jetted back to see in New York. She swung on what she called 'the trapeze' while a crowd of admiring friends colluded in the conspiracy to deceive both husbands at once.

Deirdre Bair, trying to be objective, veils her dislike and disapproval of Anaïs Nin in frequently clumsy prose. Nonetheless, for those intrigued enough by the diaries, by a writer thought to be femininity incarnate, who briefly expressed the spirit of the age, she has provided a detailed portrait. It's up to the reader to make up the story in between the lines.

JEANETTE WINTERSON

Independent on Sunday, 3 June 1995

Jeanette Winterson's sixth book *Art and Lies* takes place in the only real world its author believes fiction should evoke, that of language itself, of words on the page. Story and plot seem to have vanished; character is replaced by consciousness; narrative, such as it is, consists of strings of poetic prose, singing voices plaited together, at first sounding solo and then as a trio. *Art and Lies* signals not just its obsession with words but also its own cleverness. It comes sprinkled with long quotations in Latin, shorter ones in German and Italian, displays an implicit understanding of Greek and a familiarity with the great works of the European canon from the *Odyssey* onwards, inviting us to place Winterson at the end of a long line of famous men. Set in an eternal postmodernist present, refusing traditional notions of time, space and history, it's Winterson's most ambitious work to date. It acts as a riposte, perhaps, to those churlish critics who deemed the preceding novel, *Written on the Body*, not quite up to scratch. It even comes decorated with some pages of music as a tailpiece: the Trio from Strauss's *Der Rosenkavalier*. Winterson's trio contains Handel, Picasso and Sappho, none quite as you'd expect them to be. The Strauss extract underlines Winterson's subtitle: *A Piece for Three Voices and a Bawd*. Placed carefully at the end of the book, it reminds us, presumably in case we haven't yet worked it out, that our three narrators (the fourth, the Bawd, contributes a short wind section, or fart) blend into and out of each other, shift shape and gender at their author's whim, come harmoniously together.

The book is characterised, like all Winterson's work, by a mixture of beautiful writing, line by line shaped into original word sculptures, and moral/political denunciation of the crasser aspects of modern life. It's perhaps the presence of the latter that has helped Winterson to be placed as a prophet of the late twentieth century.

Here's a paradox: Winterson's works of art (her term) constantly insist, in a healthy structuralist way, on the primacy of the text, the words on the page. Nothing else, supposedly, counts. *Art and Lies* is prefaced by an undated quotation from one of Professor Bradley's *Oxford Lectures*: 'The nature of a work of art is to be not a part, nor yet a copy of the real world (as we commonly understand that phrase) but a world in itself, independent, complete, autonomous.' Yet at the same time Winterson's own image is of paramount importance. She has been skilfully marketed over the years, turned into an icon. A child prodigy, not just a writer of genius but also a god and guru who's glad to be gay. A fount of wisdom, an androgynous messiah dispensing profound thoughts on modern life, true love, the role of art in contemporary culture. She breaks her own rule by having it both ways.

Winterson's achievement is impressive: success, fame and fortune at a young age; total escape from the categories in which women writers are so often pigeonholed. Feminine *or* feminist *or* writes just like a man; those sidelining labels. Winterson, though writing in her first novel explicitly about lesbian desire, simultaneously distanced herself from political protesting lesbians. She suggested, right from the start, that her sexuality encouraged both her talent and her capacity to transcend ordinariness. She wasn't going to get trapped in that category of Otherness meaning Worse.

Just like many other lesbian writers, I should add, who wanted to be seen as Real Writers by a male-dominated establishment that was unable to appreciate transgressive female desire. The modernist lesbians of the twenties and thirties had to write in code, to some extent, and still have to be rescued from time to time from the lonely well of out-of-print. Jeanette Winterson asserted her desire to write of lesbianism *and* to be accepted by the literary establishment. That took courage. Lesbians, especially young ones, read and adore her. Heterosexuals are allowed a myriad idols and role models. Why shouldn't gays have as many?

I can't help wondering if the energy necessary for reading this latest book doesn't have to come from outside what it actually offers as itself, one page following another. I had to force myself to stick doggedly with it as it meandered between comments on love, life and sex in the modern world, occasional beautiful images, moral exhortations, scene-setting in cities of the mind. The pleasure of reading, of inventing and pursuing meaning, was only made possible by complete submission to the author's purpose, however rigorously concealed. Start skipping and dipping and you're lost in a maze of words refracting each other crystalline fashion. This isn't poetry, however, where you don't necessarily look for meaning. It's prose, and it's hard not to long for Ariadne's connecting thread out of the labyrinth. I am reminded of the hectic baroque of Djuna Barnes, the gleeful nonsense of Gertrude Stein. A taste, one page or two at a time, is enough. There is no compulsion to continue, to sit up all night reading in order to finish the book.

I salute Winterson's skill at word-turning and word-spinning, her capacity to mint shining images in a few golden lines, her exuberant self-confidence that lets her endlessly instruct and exhort the passive reader (Winterson doesn't give a fig for the classic advice to writers *show; don't tell*), the self-belief that allows her to write in exactly the way she wants to with no concessions to readers whinging for something a little bit more grounded, more earthed.

But. There is a but. In fact several.

Question one. What is she actually on about in *Art and Lies*?

Question two. If, as Winterson claims, 'it is the duty of every generation of writers and artists to find fresh ways of expressing the habitual circumstances of the human condition' then what exactly is her contribution to date?

Question three. Is the emperor/empress actually wearing any clothes? If he/she is not, doesn't that just prove that Winterson is a master/mistress of illusion? How tiresome, this inclusive language. Why not just call Winterson *he* and have done with it? Yet *she* on its own will hardly do, either, since, as I'll suggest further below, Winterson writes in a way that tries to defy the binary oppositions on which our civilisation supposedly rests.

To get back to the point. Let us go back to the beginning, to Winterson's first novel, *Oranges Are Not The Only Fruit*, published in 1985 by the feminist house Pandora Press.

In her 1991 introduction to the novel's reissue by Vintage (following her 'ethical decision' to leave Pandora once it was bought by Rupert Murdoch), Winterson helpfully explains to us why *Oranges* is special.

It is 'an experimental novel: its interests are anti-linear. It offers a complicated narrative structure disguised as a simple one, it employs a very large vocabulary and a beguilingly straight-forward syntax . . . *Oranges* is a threatening novel . . . a comforting novel.' Winterson also emphasises how *Oranges* is universal. This is the quality a novel must have, the conventional wisdom goes, in order to be truly great: 'Superficially, it seems specific: an evangelical household and a young girl whose world is overturned because she falls in love with another young girl. In fact, *Oranges* deals absolutely with emotions and confrontations that none of us can avoid. First love, loss, grief, rage and above all courage, these are the engines that drive the narrative through the peculiar confines of the story. Fiction needs its specifics, its anchors. It also needs to pass beyond them. It needs to be weighed down with characters we can touch and know, it also needs to fly right through them into a larger, universal space. This paradox makes work readable and durable, from its impossible tension, something harmonious is born.'

Yes and no. *Oranges* is successful precisely *because* it follows convention. It's not really written in the shape of a spiral as Winterson claims elsewhere in her Introduction. Its chapters are named after successive books of the Old Testament. It takes the traditional coming-of-age novel and the traditional feminist confessional mode of storytelling, subverts them by giving us a lesbian heroine whose version of truth (like the Bible's) may not be completely reliable, and mixes into a straightforward linear narrative some sideways digressions into myth, of the sort pioneered in the late seventies by Sara Maitland and Emma Tennant. Its great originality lies less in its supposed yoking of lesbian themes to universality than in its coupling of the coming-out-gay story to endearing wit and humour, snappy one-liners that mark the heroine's growing resistance and rebellion. Lesbian writing has not in the past crackled with jokes and ribaldry. It's been attached to discourses of passion, of tender elegy, of high camp. But not a lot of smiles. Winterson helped haul lesbians out of the well of loneliness and put them centre stage. Very cleverly, she then began to use the lesbian condition (alienation in a patriarchal society) as a launch-pad towards the romantic notion of the artist as outsider dreamed up by Shelley *et al.* Whereas for a seventies feminist telling a tale about lesbians it might have been enough to end with her heroine discovering her 'true' sexuality, for Winterson that's just the beginning.

Lesbianism denotes the possession not just of sexual proclivities but of moral and political superiority. At the end of *Oranges*, the heroine has freed herself, with pain and struggle, from mother, home, family and religion. The Christian evangelism she has abandoned has mutated into a different sense of chosenness. She confronts her former lover from whom she's been forcibly parted: 'I met her by accident, during the second year that I was away from home; she was pushing a pram. If she had been serene to the point of bovine before, she was now almost vegetable . . . she looked vague and started to discuss the weather and the roadworks and the soaring price of baby food.'

This contempt for domestic femininity is understandable, perhaps, given our culture's fear of homosexuality and vaunting of a God-given or biologically driven separation between the sexes. If lesbians are labelled monsters and perverts, as they were in the world Winterson's protagonist grew up in, then it's self-defence to fight back by refusing to accept the traditional woman's place. Perhaps that's why Winterson, despite her lesbianism, is so acceptable to her male readers. Not only is she keen on the eternal verities traditionally ascribed to the great male writers of the canon, but she articulates the anxieties about, and contempt for, femininity that characterises much modern male writing.

Contempt may mask envy. If you read Winterson's work as an ambivalent, loitering, toing and froing search that circles around questions of identity and the self, explored through love and sex, then you start to notice her interesting struggle with the feminine, now lost and now found, now inside and now outside the self, now linked to the masculine and now cut off from it.

In *The Passion*, first published in 1987, Winterson dramatised conflicts around androgyny and the shifting, relative quality of gender identity, in a carnival set in a Venice haunted by the ghosts of Italo Calvino and Angela Carter, as romantic, in its romping and cross-dressing, as anything Georgette Heyer ever dreamed up. It's a completely charming novel, a delight to read, with the intensity of fairy tale, the cool beauty of the unanalysed dream with its repression of messy feeling. It floats light as a bubble of Venetian glass, exalted, glittering. It marks the start of Winterson's use of history as a theatre backdrop to psychic drama. The Napoleonic Wars, part of its ostensible subject, are brightly coloured and two-dimensional cartoon pictures. What matters is the transitory relationship between Henri, chief chicken-cook to Napoleon's army, and the lovely adventuress Villanelle with her mysterious webbed feet. They come together and part, play lesbian and homosexual and straight, part again. Villanelle is like a vision of the anima, idealised by Henri as impossibly beautiful and therefore unattainable. He ends up imprisoned in a phallic tower from which he refuses to escape, and Villanelle returns to the fluid freedom of her beloved canals and lagoon.

Sexing the Cherry, published in 1989, repeated earlier motifs and themes, though this time the narrative hook was seventeenth-century London and voyages of discovery, the central metaphor for gender-blending was fruit grafting, and the quest for the elusive and mysterious feminine crystallised into the pursuit of a beautiful dancer, astonishingly light on her feet. The discourse on love, mediated partly by excursions into myth and fairy tale, is spoken mainly by the masculine voice. The feminine is an impossible dream that dissolves, at the book's end, into 'empty space . . . hand-shadows on the wall. Empty space and points of light.'

In *Written on the Body*, which came out in 1992, Winterson apparently changed tack, setting her genderless narrator, a very modern lover, by turns boastful, adolescent, vulnerable, potent and insecure, in contemporary London. The deeper consistency with her earlier work was twofold: the fairytale princess trapped in her tower-like house reappears, while Winterson's desire for universality and transcendence, linked to her evolving dislike of a narrative position bound up with a feminine-gendered one, made it quite logical for her not to tell us her protagonist's sex. It's an interesting experiment, of the sort pioneered by Maureen Duffy in *Love Child*, which makes the reader become active and alert to what's going on. The problem may be that the erotic scenes are less believable and less sexy because they are partially disembodied, while the narrator simply sounds like a boyish girl, with exactly the ardent naivety of all Winterson's earlier narrators. Some critics disliked the central part of the book, with its *hommage* to Monique Wittig's *Le Corps lesbien*, where the narrator gets right inside the body of the beloved. But this is less grotesque or sadistic, as some claimed, than a satisfying metaphor for a lover's hunger to enter and possess. It's associated with the heterosexual impulse, the leap back inside towards the paradise womb, but it makes perfect sense in a lesbian context too – which is what I think *Written on the Body* offers us, while it asks: when I love the body of a woman, am I man or woman or both, am I masculine or feminine, what is the difference between female and feminine, can I be both subject and object, both lover and artist?

These are the questions Winterson's *oeuvre* dramatises, questions born of the interior life of the psyche and imagination that then get mapped on to an entire cosmos, the whole of history, all the books that were ever written. They are questions that obsess every generation of young women, that Winterson asks on behalf of her readers. Her power as a writer comes partly from the originality of her prose, partly from the storytelling of its unconscious level where the anguish of adolescent female choices is battled out, the delight of adolescent female desires to be everything and give up nothing can be acted. Freud thought that women lacked penises, phallic power. Winterson's work, on one level, shows that the magic wands we seek, in a world hostile to female completeness, female creativity, have more to do with a capacity to imagine ourselves as big and bright as we want to be. In a world which frightens girls by equating femininity with constriction, self-sacrifice and lack of potency, who can blame a female hero for choosing transcendence, denial of solidarity with 'ordinary' women, the need to rise on golden wings of stern moral conviction and fly away?

Now that I've made up a story about the possible subject of *Art and Lies*, I shall go back to it and start to read it again. This time, I've got hold of a thread to guide me through the labyrinth.

SLIPSHOD SIBYLS

by Germaine Greer

Independent on Sunday, 5 October 1995

Germaine Greer's latest book pursues her interest in women's art and writing of the past shown in her two earlier works *The Obstacle Race* and *Kissing the Rod*, the one a survey of women artists and the other an anthology of seventeenth-century poetry. Now Greer moves on to consider the poets themselves, some of them newly canonised by feminist scholars but the whole bunch splenetically condemned by Alexander Pope as the slipshod sibyls of Greer's title, badly coiffed and sloppily dressed. His metaphor collapsed two criticisms into a single indictment of femininity: they were poetesses who did not know their poetics and cared less.

Greer has in fact written three books in one. The first is an intervention into the battle waged on campuses about women's studies, whether the traditional male-dominated canon of Great Writers needs to be overhauled or dismantled, whether feminist scholars are correct in resurrecting forgotten female poets or whether they're motivated by ignorant sentimentality. Greer's second book, around which the first is fitted as a polemical prologue and epilogue, is a series of essays providing textual analysis and close readings of the works of these women poets, from Sappho onwards. It concentrates on the sixteenth to the nineteenth centuries and offers a sharp look at the myths informing our appreciation of, for example, Aphra Behn or Christina Rossetti. The third book is a discussion of the moral and ideological climate in which women tried to write, hampered by lack of education and deeply enshrined notions of sexual difference which set in after the Renaissance and insisted on the poet as male in love with an impregnating female muse. Linking these three books into one is a marvellously passionate critique of the way our culture has so severely divided women from men, to the grief of both. A battle-cry constantly surfaces, descant-like, in the text, on behalf of women unable sufficiently to mutilate their souls to qualify as truly, deeply, madly feminine in patriarchy's terms. She throws plenty of scorn at those lady poets she deems foolish failures, who presumably would have done better to stick to pudding-making and stocking-mending, but she has plenty of sympathy for any woman struggling less against the fact of her sex than against the constraints of conventional ideas of gender. Pope's slipshod sibyls sneer, she tartly points out, could apply to both sorts of women: 'The term is weighted with all the contempt expressed by literary men for literary women who took themselves seriously, who risked ridicule, exploitation and calumny because they thought they had something to say, and the contempt likewise meted out to the women who fooled around with poetry, who did not try hard enough or fell for the fiction that poetry can come easily.'

Greer's main thesis acts as a corrective to some feminist wishful thinking: 'The more we know about women who wrote poetry in English before 1900, the more we must realise that it is not a question of women poets having been ignored or obscured but of women's poetry remaining unwritten because women were disabled and deflected by the great tradition itself, while a select band of arbitrarily chosen token women, all young, beautiful and virtuous, were rewarded for their failures. Second-rate, dishonest, fake poetry is worse than no poetry at all. To insist on equal representation or positive discrimination so that She-poetry appears on our syllabuses in our schools and universities is to continue the system of false accounting that produced the double standard in the first place. This is not to say that we should not work at reclaiming women's work but simply that we should be aware that we are more likely to find heroines than poets.' This is certainly true of Greer's own *Kissing the Rod*, in which the potted biographies of those earlier poets are often more gripping than the poems themselves.

The great tradition Greer cites, which demanded a classical education, a thorough immersion in Greek and Latin poetics, could, however, be hard on men too. The eighteenth century, especially, produced reams of dreary bombastic heroic couplets by both sexes, whose clumping fake classicism makes one want to scream with boredom, whose twittering rhymes are turgid and repellent. When Blake comes into view at the end of the century you cry out with gratitude. Can *écriture féminine*, authentic female voices in poetry, be invented without the benefits of higher education? Greer does not explore this point. What of unlettered, self-taught male poets? Did they too feel forced to write in an alien tradition? She does not say.

Though so many women failed to make it on male terms as real poets, others did have success with the novel. You can see language being bent and twisted and reshaped in the early novel, and its female exponents, in from the start, were agile and adept. Was this because the novel employed literary forms closer to female experience, like the letter, the confession, the tale of horror or intrigue?

Once she has disposed of the troops of inept poetesses, however, Greer in fact concentrates on women poets first established as interesting and important by Cora Kaplan in her ground-breaking study *Salt and Bitter and Good*. She clearly does think *some* women wrote well, even if only the elite few who combined learning with wit and some kind of sexual confidence. Her argument can't fail to provoke contemporary echoes, in our age of creative writing classes and local poetry groups and self-publishing, of fights about whether feminist aesthetics can or should exist, of whether male poets should be called such, of whether being a self-declared female poet is the same as believing in essentially feminine creativity. Greer's descriptions of Regency and early Victorian literary London, in which the unfortunate Letitia Landon launched herself as a writer of execrable verse whose initial success depended on her self-presentation as Childe Bimbo out of Byron–Goethe–Rousseau, reverberate for us today when publicists try to present women poets as Living Dolls (while male poets still have to imitate Mr Rochester or toy suggestively with pipes or rifles); if you're not sexy, pretty or young, forget it; until you turn sixty and can be repackaged as a sibyl, slipshod or not.

Things were not always so bad, however. Greer's early chapter 'The Transvestite Poet' discusses the Renaissance as a time of relative freedom from oppressive stereotypes, when the constricting corset of femininity could be gaily worn by either sex, when Rosalind could wear breeches for a quick saunter and swagger, in a carnivalesque moment producing an outpouring of great poetry. Greer quotes the Italian women writers who could speak of their desire as fearlessly as any man, just as they could speak in a male persona if they so desired, or in both at once, or in neither. The Elizabethans, Greer argues, saw sexuality as playful, womanish, childish, boyish. They valued lots of different kinds of pleasure and routes to it, and didn't think of women as less desiring than men. Interestingly, the English poets Greer quotes to support this view are male: Shakespeare, Jonson, *et al.* We reach the epitome of female gallantry with Restoration wit Aphra Behn; after her time sexual divisions began to close in and the feminine brain and sensibility to be invented. Sex was out; domestic affections were in. There's a strong suggestion, not spelled out, that if women are denied sexual knowledge and potency then our writing suffers. Repression leads to clichés.

Sappho has been repressed, Greer argues, by myth-makers eager to transform her into the exception that proves the rule: the brilliant and perfect poet with whom no other woman dare compete. A *monstre sacré* used for scaring women off, just as the Virgin Mary, getting pregnant without sex, has been used to make us guilty about our bodies and our sexuality, badly in need of redemption. In fact, Sappho exists mainly as holes in papyrus, and the gaps have been filled in by all sorts of artists masquerading as scholars, so that down the centuries, according to the whims of fashion, Sappho has metamorphosed into ladylike muse, feminist icon, or lesbian kitsch object of the Alma Tadema variety, a perverse idol for men who liked their beautiful women dead. The invention of the myth of Sappho's Leap, in which, though deeply lesbian, she kills herself for love of a man, largely contributed, Greer insists, to the cult of female poetic suicide in the twentieth century, the pawky idea that the best woman poet is a self-immolated one. This chapter, rich in quotation in Greek, is hard going for anyone who hasn't learned the language, but it is rewarding nonetheless.

From Sappho Greer leaps to the Restoration, to 'what has passed down to us as the authentic work of Katherine Philips' which turns out to be a mess of probably unauthorised revisions made by others, in some cases so substantial as to be virtual rewritings. Though Philips is a recognised major poet of her time: 'yet only now are academics beginning to invest energy and resources in establishing her text . . . Feminist scholars who clamour for women's work to be included in the canon assume that there are texts attributed to women that actually represent what women wrote and the way they wrote it. The further back we go from our own time, the more unlikely that is.' The problem is exacerbated with Aphra Behn. Greer suggests that our insistence on seeing her as Puss in Boots swinging up from Kent to make her fortune in the big smoke obscures the painful reality of life for literary hacks at the time. Men and women worked in conditions of near slavery and dire poverty, and Behn, Greer dares to insist, probably *did* live off male protectors, since the sexual double standard could not be bypassed. If we see Behn as a driven survivor in terms of her biography, then we might also see that she was an expert user and rewriter of others' bad plays. Greer makes a good case for Behn as ghost-writer, not only ripping off the plot and language of Thomas Killigrew's *Thomaso* for her own smash hit *The Rover*, but actually writing *Thomaso* to Killigrew's dictation, since he was probably illiterate. This is a wonderful tale, a chapter full of marvellous flourishes, bluffs and counter-bluffs, but which doesn't obscure the bleak implications of Behn's harsh battle with sexual disease and penury. She was not, Greer implies, the heroine that some of us have wanted her to be, but she was a fine and wily writer. Similar misapprehensions cloud our view, she tells us, of Anne Wharton, Rochester's niece, whose poetry in fact constantly pays homage to him as guide and preceptor and must not be read as the naive outpourings of her sweet young heart, since she was an intelligent libertine herself. Then there's the case of the great William Wordsworth, publishing the work of Lady Winchilsea and editing it so badly that it comes to us in severely curtailed and rewritten form. We move on to Christina Rossetti, who receives a drubbing for allowing her brother Gabriel to suggest alterations in her work, and for being such a neurotic Christian that she constantly sabotages herself. This was Virginia Woolf's conclusion too.

In her quick tour of the twentieth century and its dreary list of female poets' suicides, Greer moves back into polemical mode, castigating these women, whose suffering was undoubtedly real, for not behaving better and just snapping out of it. An acknowledgement of unconscious processes, and their inaccessibility to simple exhortations to good sense, would give her greater compassion. Greer asserts that writing poetry became associated with making a career out of suicide, that neurotic women wanted to write bad exhibitionistic verse as a rehearsal for dying. But personalities made less robust than Greer's by childhood wounds that remain open and unreachable in the unconscious, the wounds of fantasy being as severe as the wounds of 'fact', may seek to heal themselves through the writing of poetry. We shouldn't expect our women poets to be saints. A poet is simply *femme moyenne sensuelle.* Marina Tsvetayeva may well have been masochistic and controlling as a person, but she wrote some marvellous poetry, if we trust Elaine Feinstein's beautiful translations. Equally, with Sylvia Plath and Anne Sexton, you could argue that the psychic wound, whatever it was, which produced the neurosis, simultaneously functioned to open up a route to the unconscious, contact with which is necessary for writing real poetry. Perhaps in repressed, hygienic, fifties New England culture, creativity could only emerge, initially, by that painful route. But then both got on with the hard graft of becoming professional poets, redrafting endlessly, sharply self-critical; tough workers. That they both wrote so much about female damage, as well as about other subjects, is simply an indictment of the century in which we live, still shadowed by Christianity's horrible doctrine of the Atonement, belief in suffering as a virtue, and creed of female self-abnegation. Quibbles apart, this is a valuable and fascinating book, crucial reading for all who love women and poetry and desire them to go together better in the future.

'TRADITION AND THE INDIVIDUAL TALENT'

by T. S. Eliot

Lecture given at the Voice Box, South Bank Centre, London, 1 October 1996

The language of theory and of literary criticism ages far more quickly than the language of poetry and novels, perhaps because the theories themselves go out of fashion so fast and are replaced by something new. It's hard work wading through the works of most nineteenth-century and early twentieth-century critics, whereas the fiction and verse of their contemporaries, the good ones at any rate, stay lively and fresh. It may have something to do with the style that many critics adopt: stiff, pompous, preachy. Morality creeps in; the superego takes over. Whereas novels and poetry, inspired by the subversively creative id, allow the drives of desire full rein. Theory often seems to be about control, using a language that classifies, pigeonholes, restrains, inhibits the subject under review. Poetry flies in the opposite direction, opening things up, confusing and mixing categories through its use of metaphor, piling one reality on top of another and altering both. Literary theory tends, sooner or later, to wither away. I don't expect the language of this lecture to last very long, either. It's disposable art. If it serves to encourage you to go away and read some of the poets I'm going to mention later on, particularly perhaps those that you may not have come across before, then I shall be happy.

When I read 'Tradition and the Individual Talent' for the first time, a few weeks ago, I was put off by its chilly, superior tone. Reading it felt like quite hard work. I had to reach beyond my own dislike and prejudice to get at the ideas. T. S. Eliot himself was well aware of the difficulties posed to readers by the style of his essays. In 'To Criticize the Critic', a lecture delivered at Leeds University in 1961, he looked back over his own career as a writer of criticism and pointed out that the language of his essays, especially his early ones, was characterised by 'the occasional note of arrogance, of vehemence, of cocksureness or rudeness, the braggadocio of the mild-mannered man safely entrenched behind his typewriter'.

'Tradition and the Individual Talent', considered by many to be one of Eliot's most important essays, is also one of his first, published in 1919 in *The Egoist.* If it swaggers and lays down the law, well, perhaps that's all we can expect of youth, when doubts and subtlety are so often overlaid by supreme self-confidence. I think there are other problems with the language, however, which belong with its 'arrogance' and 'cocksureness' and it's these on which I shall be focusing here.

But first of all it's necessary to ask: what's 'Tradition and the Individual Talent' all about? If, like me, you are not *au fait* to your fingertips with Eliot's works of criticism, perhaps you might appreciate a précis. My reading is, of course, a subjective one, and so this résumé is too.

Eliot's essay re-evaluates the idea of tradition as important or not to poets and argues that a sense, or knowledge, of tradition is crucial to writing well. A mature poet, a good poet, absorbs past poetry as part of being an individual; the past is part of the present, and is modified by it. Following on from this, Eliot asserts that what is really modern and new is to be aware of, and consciously part of, the ever-changing 'mind of Europe'. To allow this integration with the body of European poetry to happen, a poet must undergo a sort of death, the death of personality, at least. The poet must become a medium for absorbing and transforming material. The result is a poem, a piece of art, which depends on its own complexity and worth to be a good and satisfying piece of work, not on that of the emotions or sufferings of the person who wrote the poem. The poem has to stand by itself, justify itself, on its own. We can't plead that because we felt so much or so strongly that therefore we have written a good poem. The poem must be judged as a poem. Eliot makes a further distinction between poetic value and anything smacking of ethics. It's not what we say so much as how we say it. It's no good having beautiful and good thoughts if we express them in bad poetry. It's not our feelings that matter; it's the poem. That's why the doctrine of impersonality becomes so important for Eliot. He sums up in conclusion: 'The emotion of art is impersonal. And the poet cannot reach this impersonality without surrendering himself wholly to the work to be done. And he is not likely to know what *is* to be done unless he lives in what is not merely the present, but the present moment of the past, unless he is conscious, not of what is dead, but of what is already living.'

High-falutin though this may sound, Eliot, here, was not in fact preaching an elitist doctrine. He recognised that the 'usual objection' would be brought against him, that 'the doctrine requires a ridiculous amount of erudition (pedantry)'. Far from it, Eliot asserted:

> While, however, we persist in believing that a poet ought to know as much as will not encroach upon his necessary receptivity and necessary laziness, it is not desirable to confine knowledge to whatever can be put into a useful shape for examinations, drawing rooms, or the still more pretentious modes of publicity. Some can absorb

> knowledge, the more tardy must sweat for it. Shakespeare acquired more essential history from Plutarch than most men could from the whole British Museum.

There are many good things in this essay, provocative, encouraging, consoling to the lover of poetry whether reader or writer or both. It's heartening to be reminded that we must feed our imaginations by wide reading, for example. I would add, however, that it is crucial to read not only the poetry of the past but also the poetry of the present. As someone who has judged quite a few poetry competitions and has taught quite a few creative writing and poetry classes, I have noticed how many aspiring poets rarely read any poetry written in the last twenty years, unless they are very young, in which case they may *only* know about rap poetry or dub poetry or the latest thing in performance work, and may consider they have little to learn in any case. People who don't read modern poetry yet produce poems are often making work which is fossilised, written in the styles of earlier periods as though these can simply be reproduced (like reproduction furniture), as though there were no necessity to make translations into the idiom of our own time. These poems have no guts or life. They don't engage with the vernacular, which modern poetry must do, even though it will not necessarily copy it. Poetry today uses some version of a speaking voice. Anyone aping the written styles of, for example, the Georgian poets, in this day and age, is not going to sound convincing. I would argue, therefore, that a good modern poet must be as aware of contemporary work as of work from the past. It's a pity Eliot doesn't specifically discuss the invention of the poetic voice. His entire essay is a defence of the modern works written by himself and his friends, but he doesn't go into any detail about how the new poetic idiom is forged. In our day, the ideological battle is fought out, in the pages of the media at least, in simplistic terms:

either you love Bob Dylan *or* you love Keats. Nonsense. You'll be a better poet for loving both, or at least reading both.

The real problems that I have with this essay are to do with Eliot's use of the term 'tradition', and one of the implications of his doctrine of impersonality. Let's say I wouldn't put things quite as he does. To explain why, I shall have to become personal. Rather than embarking here on a lengthy defence of subjectivity as part of critical response, I shall let that emerge in the course of my discussion. The points I want to make are all interlinked, but I'll present them one by one, in an attempt at clarity. What I'm offering you is not so much a reasoned argument, rigorous and integrated, as a series of puzzles and questions to most of which I don't know the answer but hope you might.

To begin with something as simple as a pronoun. You may have noticed that when summarising Eliot's essay I referred to the poet as 'the poet' or as 'we'. You may also have noticed, in the extract I read of Eliot's own words, that in these the poet is always referred to as 'he'. A conventional usage, you may say, that I shouldn't quibble at, oh dear these irritating and boring feminists who simply cannot believe that *we* are contained in *him* quite safely and adequately, just as Eve was made out of Adam's rib. As long as our language contains the feminine and diminutive version 'poetess', I shall continue to believe that Eliot's 'poet' defines the male poet and excludes the female one. *Can* a male poet carry a female one inside himself? Is it not the woman who conceives, carries and delivers the male? What does it do to a woman poet's sense of her capabilities and capacities to read literary criticism in which poets are referred to as *he* and in which the only poets mentioned are male ones? I think you might have to be a woman poet to answer that. We are beginning to make our answer, at the level of criticism and at the level of poetry, and we are beginning to ask those people who continue to say only *he* to try and imagine how we feel.

Women poets who cling to the notion of male superiority, who are only able to value masculine creation because they have imbibed so much of the self-hatred common to women in this women-fearing culture, continue not to object to being referred to as *he*, to de-sex themselves, to think I'm whinging and making a silly fuss. They will tell me that the true poet is androgynous. I shall reply that in that case *he* is not an adequate pronoun. The fact remains that when I read this essay by Eliot I'm not absolutely convinced that he is including me in his discussion of what makes a modern poet. Clearly, I have not sufficiently put into practice the doctrine of impersonality.

Eliot insists on how we need to extinguish ourselves in order to take in the past. He says of the poet: 'What happens is a continual surrender of himself as he is at the moment to something which is more valuable. The progress of an artist is a continual self-sacrifice, a continual extinction of personality.' I can recognise that 'surrender' and 'extinction', certainly. I think we experience them in the rapture of reading and in the rapture of writing, when the conscious self, the ego, dissolves, and we sink down into the level of language that's below speech and find words there that we bring up and put on to paper – or on to our word-processor screens. Eliot, though in this essay he is completely unclear about his usage of the terms 'emotions' and 'feelings', does come up with the idea of the poet's mind as some kind of receptacle for all kinds of impressions, thoughts, images and sensations, and indeed those emotions and feelings he wants to distinguish from each other but does not manage to. You might call this the bowl model of creativity. The imagination, or mind, is an inner space (men can have one too), a crucible in which the poem is forged. And at the same time, contradictorily, Eliot asserts that the poet's mind is the catalyst in the bowl, the neutral component that causes a chemical reaction in which it plays no direct part, just as two particular gases, mixed in the presence of a filament of platinum, will form sulphurous acid. 'The more perfect the artist', Eliot says, 'the more completely separate in him will be the man who suffers and the mind which creates; the more perfectly will the mind digest and transmute the passions which are its material.' So now the mind has become a sort of mouth, stomach and digestive tract. This muddle of images suggests to me an emotional difficulty involved in trying to think about creativity. No wonder. Which of us can say we've got it right, understood it perfectly? I am certainly not criticising Eliot for sounding confused. I don't, however, feel that he has convinced me that in order to take in the past you must first obliterate yourself. How do you know what you have taken in if you don't know, to start with, what you've already got? Or what you haven't got but long for? Or what you have been deprived of and desperately need? Eliot seems to think that all these great, beautiful nourishing works of the past arrive with labels on confirming their excellence. Who put those labels on? A critic up in the sky called God? For Eliot the excellence of works of art is self-evident and obvious. Yet the history of reading and writing poetry is also the history of creating, erasing and reshaping canons and traditions. If you look at the problems through gender spectacles it becomes clear that 'impersonality' is in fact denial. You need to know you are a woman in order to realise that many women writers have been left out of the canon, the received notion of the tradition, of poetry. It is notably not male writers who have criticised the canon's built-in bias, but female ones. 'Impersonality' here means it is in men's interests not to notice. It is in fact a *masculine* doctrine. I'm not suggesting that Eliot was cooking up conspiracy theory to exclude women poets from Parnassus. I think he was impregnated with the prejudices of his time and that these are *part* of his being a great poet, not separate from it. But my sense of tradition is different from his, because I am a woman poet not a male one. Virginia Woolf wrote wonderfully well about this. She suggested that the view of the terrain is different if you spend your time looking out from the top of a tower. The people on the ground will see things differently, and will also be willing to assert that the tower does indeed exist. The people in the tower may not be able to see the ground at all.

The bridge between Eliot's view of impersonality and my own, in this aspect concerning our attitude towards tradition, could be the word 'unconscious', though, if you want to look at it another way, it might be functioning as a fence with spikes on top. I find some of Freud's ideas helpful for thinking about how the imagination works, whereas I don't think that Eliot does. But Eliot does seem to be suggesting that the action of the creative mind is utterly mysterious and immensely powerful, just as a Freudian would assert our unconscious life can be, and that what we call the personal self, the daily ego that huffs and puffs, hustles and bustles, is just the tip of the iceberg. Down there under the water is something bigger that we know less about. *Perhaps* Eliot is suggesting that.

What I am suggesting, in any case, is that a sense of personal rather than impersonal, existence and history is necessary for discovering the tradition that will nourish us as poets. It's my contention, as it's been my experience, that the tradition is made by human hands, not those of God, that it's quarrelled over and renewed generation by generation, and that it has reflected the tastes and preferences of powerful groups. As Anne Elliot says in *Persuasion* to Captain Harville: 'the pen has been in *your* hands'. Women, only allowed into public education in the last hundred years, have not been in charge of deciding what the tradition consists of. Things have changed enormously in the last twenty years. Young women who are poets are much thicker on the ground. A lot of their battles are fought. They can write about whatever they like. They don't have to take a lot of notice of their gender if they don't want to, so confident is this younger generation of its equality with men that it goes without saying. When I was a young poet, women poets were the exceptions who proved the rule. Stereotypes abounded: the woman poet was hysterical, neurotic, comically spinsterish, *dead*. My generation had the exhilarating task, which was a painful struggle at times, of discovering an ignored and forgotten tradition of female writers that we could plait into the male one we knew so much more about. We read voraciously, as I'm sure Eliot himself would have wished, but we read the women he and his generation of poets ignored. Yes, Pound appreciated Hilda Doolittle as a fine Imagist poet, but nonetheless he renamed and de-sexed her as H.D. She's one example of an ignored genius. Put her epic poetry alongside Eliot's and see them mutually re-ignite. It's a disgrace that schoolchildren are automatically pointed towards *The Waste Land* but never *Helen in Egypt*. Our culture can't support the feminine as a sign of greatness in poetry, that's why. Femininity, in 1919, was too restrictive. It's that simple. To survive, a woman had to become eccentric, or bisexual, or lesbian, or odd, in the history of modernism. Look how Anna Wickham got written off and written out, or Charlotte Mew. Tell me that those two aren't as good as any of the Georgian men still taking up space in the anthologies and I'll challenge you to a duel. Those poetry anthologies, before 1970, are stuffed with men. Very few women. Thanks to the efforts of feminist writers, editors, publishers and scholars, who braved ridicule and contempt and managed on very little money, the history of literature, and in this case specifically the history of poetry, got rewritten. People started jumping on the bandwagon, because these new books sold. The establishment publishers started bringing out their own anthologies of women's poetry. Forgive me if I sound cynical. I think they were less eager to shake up the old divisive categories of masculine and feminine than to sell a few books. They always chose female editors who weren't feminists but . . .

What I want to say here, to T. S. Eliot and to any doubters among my listeners, is that it's difficult completely to imagine how it feels to be excluded from the tradition (to Eliot's credit, he wasn't arguing for a narrow canon of 'excellence' but for the wealth of books available) unless it's happened to you. It's difficult to imagine how wary and leery that can you make feel of tradition, if you feel that you don't belong, that you're exiled from culture, you're the barbarian at the gates, you're what's been rubbed out and shut up. I'm not in the slightest bit surprised, actually, despite what I said earlier about the importance of reading as widely as possible if you want to write well, that so many beginner poets, particularly those who haven't been to university and received the notion that they *do* belong in the culture, they *can* inherit the tradition, are afraid of reading the poetry of the past. Although I had a privileged education, going to Oxford, writing poetry was something I did in secret. I was a member of the Poetry Society, which did not, in my three years of membership, ever invite a female poet to come and read. Its male members to whom I read my poetry said: oh you poor dear you're so *bitter*. What kept me going as a poet? Desire and anger. Personal qualities, I'm afraid. It's possible to feel that the poetry of the tradition annihilates you, if you don't feel that you belong in that tradition. It's possible to have very mixed feelings about it. To follow your own vision takes enormous courage, and for this you need the support of a peer group in so far as that's possible and not just an idealistic dream. Once your own vision has achieved some bit of recognition, it's much easier to start to read the others' version of their tradition. Once I'd nourished myself, over ten years or so of writing, on the women poets being made available to me by the publishing practices of the seventies, I felt strong enough to go back to the male poets I'd loved as an adolescent. It was rather like loving my mother, realising I did love my father however patriarchal he could sometimes be, then putting them together as a couple and realising what they'd both given me. But I had to go in search of my mother, and of the literary tradition that embodied her. She wasn't there as my birthright. She was hidden. I had no female model for becoming a poet. I had to find one, make one up. I had to discover and invent a tradition that allowed me to become a poet. I had to imagine a maternal body made of words and milk and music and permissiveness and fierceness and sweetness and power and and and. This invisible woman became my muse. In the past men named women as muses and themselves as poets. I know that we women can be both, muses and poets both; if you love women you can be inspired and write, and that goes for both sexes, and for gay and straight.

I should like to add that this sense of being excluded from the tradition gave me a sense of solidarity with other groups who, for different reasons, may not feel completely comfortable with their relationship to the Eliot-defined tradition, either. Modernist art was often inspired by, and eagerly borrowed from, cultures outside the European one, though it did not always acknowledge this. At a time when the English language, and literature in English, is being greatly enriched and reinvigorated by those of its citizen-poets who can draw on, for example, Caribbean or Asian imagery and idiom, it seems unambitious to talk only of European literature, European poems, as Eliot does, when our past tradition, that future generations will inherit, is already so deeply rooted in so many different cultures and ways of putting poems together. Perhaps we should think about tradition as not only pointing back towards the past but also forwards to the future. Certainly it is becoming increasingly connected to the art of translation. Equally certainly it is shaped by publishing budgets and government subsidies, by bureaucratic decisions about what children may read at school. It is not solid, not easily knowable. It changes shape, shifts about. It's not God-given, simply out there waiting for us to take it in. It's made by human beings, out of human quarrels about what's good and deserves to be read. Human scholarship helps us to understand the process of preserving or distorting the texts of poems. For example, now that great quantities of poetry by women of the seventeenth and eighteenth centuries have finally been collected up and published in massive anthologies, we can at last read it and quarrel over whether any of these poems are any good and deserve to have lasted (and yes, you discover that just as, for example, there were an awful lot of boring poems written by men in the eighteenth century, so there were an awful lot of boring ones written by women too). Germaine Greer has recently pointed out that women poets of the past were sabotaged not only by being denied education, by being told that women were muses not poets, by the sexual double standard which muffled women's free speech, by early deaths in childbed, by being bowdlerised or sloppily edited, by being turned into fashionable freaks famous merely for being feminine, but also, sometimes, by simply not writing well enough. Now, while I will defend to my last breath Dr Greer's right to criticise as weak or inept some of the poets she has herself anthologised, I want to be allowed to make my own judgement. The crucial point is that at least I am now able to read these poems, because they are beginning to exist in reliable texts, and so I can make up my mind. Once you find you've got many more foremothers than you ever dreamed, you can stop being amazed, *à la* Dr Johnson, that woman can do it all, and get on with the business of reading and writing. But first of all you need the poems of the past to exist, solid and real, in books.

The structure of my essay so far has reflected my process of reading Eliot's: circling around, puzzling over what he might have meant, answering back, shooting off at tangents. I want to conclude by trying to explain one aspect of my own aesthetic, to clarify my response to Eliot's and mark where we differ.

While I would agree with Eliot that writing a poem is not simple self-expression, and the finished poem cannot be read back to the writer as a way of validating it but must stand or fall on its own, I see a connection between the poet and the poem, during the process of creation, and a connection between the person who suffers (or experiences bliss) and the person who writes the poem. These are two aspects of one person; I don't see them as split from each other, and the more severely split the better, but as in contact. Sometimes they're fighting, sometimes they're doing a tango, sometimes they are mother and baby, sometimes they're lovers, but they are always in relationship to each other. One of my images for the imagination, or as Eliot calls it the poet's mind, is like his: a container. For me, memory is a crucial part of imagining. The past is inside us. The personal past, of our childhoods, lives on inside us. This is very similar to Eliot's view that the past is crucially part of the present, crucially affecting it, except that I think that the personal past is just as valuable to the poet as the 'impersonal' one, the tradition of which Eliot speaks. In fact, I find it very hard to believe that I can take in the European past, so to speak, while simultaneously repressing my own personal experience of my own past. It seems to me that the past of a person and the past of Europe (to use Eliot's chosen continent) are probably profoundly and inextricably linked, and that exploring how and why this should be so could help with the writing of poetry, not necessarily hinder it. The stiff upper lip position in this country has always been that it's bad form, self-indulgent, *wrong*, to think too much about your feelings and understand or express them. Doing so will lead to floods of self-expression, oh horror, and the gushing of terrible poetry. It all depends on how you look at it, what model of self and world you use. Peter Redgrove once remarked (I can't remember his exact words) that if the human psyche is part of the universe then exploring the psyche means exploring the universe. The problem vanishes. Similarly, you could say that if we are part of history, then the personal past makes part of the European one. Excavating tradition, searching for it in the way I described earlier, might therefore also involve searching for one's own past, one's own memories. Memory is a series of fictions. So, perhaps, is history. These stories, these artefacts, these narrative poems, exist not only 'out there' but also 'in here'.

Eliot placed poetry firmly outside the self, beyond it, separate from it. Rather snootily, he says that only those who *have* personality and emotions can know what it is to need to escape from them (the idea being that poets are more sensitive sufferers than the rest of humanity). He can then, it seems to me, distance himself from anything nasty in the poem and anything nasty in himself. He uses as an example some lines by Tourneur, which exhibit, he thinks, a peculiar blend of attraction and disgust, what Frank Kermode has called 'a mortuary eroticism balancing on the moment of simultaneous enchantment and loss, the sexual surrender', beauty all tangled up with what Eliot calls 'the ugliness which is contrasted with it and which destroys it'. Eliot goes to some lengths to explain that the force of these lines comes from themselves, not merely from their position in the dramatic structure of the play. But surely, to create these lines, Tourneur had to imagine the sexual ambivalence of the man who utters them? Had to create these feelings inside himself? Eliot refers instead to 'floating feelings' – conveniently *outside*. Was he, perhaps, unwilling to admit that *he* could ever be capable of feeling violent sexual ambivalence towards women's bodies, a mixture of desire and disgust? Conflicting feelings are, after all, extremely difficult for us to tolerate. One way of dealing with them might be to project them into another place, called a poem, and then to create an aesthetic denying any connection between self and poem. The poem (like Tourneur's lines) might be very beautiful while also, simultaneously, articulating unpleasant feelings and views. Perhaps there's a parallel here with the debate currently raging about whether or not Eliot was anti-Semitic and whether or not proof of this can be found in his poems. Eliot's own aesthetic lets him off the hook, since the poem has nothing to do with the poet and is not an expression of the poet's feelings. A different view might lead us to suggest that putting what appear to be anti-Semitic lines into a poem means, at the very least, that the poet was capable of imagining them. What interests me, here, is how convenient the doctrine of impersonality becomes, as a psychological defence against nasty thoughts. You see the unconscious operating, to blot out the links between self and poem, though for Eliot this was the mysterious way in which art moved, mysterious as the ways of God to man.

What's the point, though, of remembering the personal past, of allowing and watching and discovering its operation in the present? How can this help the writing of poetry? Perhaps it doesn't. Not in any obvious sense, anyway. All I can tell you is what I have discovered. Having found out that memory and the imagination are crucially linked inside some kind of 'inner space' I have come to see that the process of creation involves the process of repairing. Remembering is re-membering (as Mary Daly, Adrienne Rich and Melanie Klein, all in their own ways, have pointed out). I have come to see how my 'outer' search for a tradition of poetry-writing in which I can belong and feel welcome, which I can help to make fuller and more representative by my reading and studying, has been matched by my 'inner' search, my quest to re-member: to find what I lost, to re-energise, mend, put back together, something beloved and important that has been missing or damaged or destroyed. A body. A body of knowledge. A body of love. Inner and outer worlds are connected by the image of the mother, the absent one gone underground, whom the daughter searches for. The child I was, in my story of my personal past, believed she had damaged that mother, driven her away, perhaps killed her, with her greed and rage, her sexual fantasies, her jealous love for Dad. The daughter I am, in my story of my search in history, thinks that patriarchy hides, disguises, idealises, denigrates, damages the figure of that mother. The poem seems to be the acknowledgement of my own anger for that mother, my love for her, my sorrow at her disappearance. It is my search for her. It is my finding her again; our reunion; my mending of what was damaged. My myth has its roots in the Middle East, in northern Africa, in Greece, in Palestine, as it has its roots in my heart, in the deepest places inside me. Writing a poem enacts the myth, makes me part of history, part of the world, joins the inner and outer senses of self. It acts out metaphor, as I take the language I have inherited from tradition and family, the language of poets and the language of my parents, as I break up that language and destroy it then reassemble it, through the finding of poetic form, into a new pattern of words. Writing a poem, putting words together, is thus profoundly reparative, and the experience of writing a poem is indeed blissful, the joyful, strange act of surrender that Eliot called 'the bewildering minute', whether the process lasts, in 'reality', five minutes or a day. That minute is a golden minute, like mystical experience, when we and the world become one.

4

On Reading

READING GENEROUSLY

Virago supplement in the *Guardian*, 7 June 1997

As adults, we can take language for granted, but when you're a child you see how extraordinary it is, this flow of sounds, these words that are both separate and connected. I had trouble learning to read, and can remember sitting on the floor in front of the book-case in the front room of my parents' house, staring at the books behind the glass panes of the doors and trying to imagine what they contained. Then, suddenly, I could read them. We children had our own shelves of Blackie's Children's Classics upstairs, but I liked nosing through my parents' books which were all mixed up together. They both read novels. My father liked Dornford Yates and C. S. Forrester's Hornblower series, and my mother had Alfred de Musset and Pierre Loti in brightly coloured paper bindings. My mother was too busy to have much time for reading for fun, but she read doggedly through the French *nouveaux romans* for the A Level French classes she taught, keeping herself up to date. I loved her story of how, as a girl, she read Diderot's *La Réligieuse* and then, when she'd finished it, hurled it across the room. This was said with flashing eyes. She and Dad discussed what they read, as they discussed everything else, with vehemence and passion. My grandmother, who lived with us, also read a great deal, getting novels out of the public library. She once shamed me in front of some university friends I'd hoped to impress by boasting to them that I was a great reader and loved the books of Georgette Heyer, didn't I, dear? I, who pretended to read nothing but medieval poetry, blushed with mortification. I was well aware, by then, of segregated and secret reading. It was an odd and lopsided literary set-up in those days. Great literature was for everybody, and was written by dead men, only of course we never thought about that in 1967. Romantic novels, read and written by women, were considered trash. That was that.

Twenty years of feminist publishing have changed our perceptions of what can be written about and by whom. Young writers now claim a freedom to write about whatever they please, just as they claim sexual confidence and ease, and this is surely partly owing to feminism (whether they feel grateful or not) as it's also partly about late capitalism's appetite for raunchy writing by stroppy girls: a new market has been opened up. Gender does not necessarily matter any more, since we're supposedly living in a post-feminist age, all problems solved and all avenues open; or else, in certain circumstances, it's a selling point. Have all the old contradictions around women and writing really withered away, or have they merely been swept under the postmodern carpet? Do men and women now write fiction in the same way, or are there differences? Why do more women than men read novels? Why do so many men not want to bother with reading novels and consider fiction less important than biography or political gossip?

Jane Austen was no explicit feminist, though she wrote brilliantly about women's strategic manoeuvrings for financial and domestic power through marriage, but her novels explore some of these issues, because they were as much debated in her day as in ours. I'd love to think of her sitting up late into the night talking with Mary Wollstonecraft and Madame de Staël about the life of the imagination but, alas, there's no hint their paths ever crossed. Except via books. She clearly experienced, through her reading, dramatic encounters with some of the greatest and most popular writers of her time, and records the impact on her of contemporary fiction with both affection and mockery. Re-reading *Northanger Abbey* recently, I was struck by how up to date it seemed. Catherine Morland, the heroine, is a great reader. Not of history, though. She declares to Henry Tilney, the young man she's in love with, that she dislikes reading history because there are so few women in it. Novels, on the other hand, are founded on the lives of women, and Catherine reads these in plenty. She is aware of the low status that novels have, for the reason that they are so intimately connected with the female sex, and apologises to Henry for being so fond of them and devouring so many. To her amazement, he sticks up for novels and declares that he loves the Gothic variety, which he reads with his hair standing on end the entire time. Jane Austen has a lot of fun teasing Catherine for taking her beloved novels too literally, for supposing that the hair-raising adventures befalling their heroines are *real*, rather than make-believe. To the modern, post-Freudian reader, Catherine's reading is a valid one. The Gothic tales she so loves do describe a reality: the reality of the psyche, of the inner world, of the unconscious imagination, where parts of ourselves we suppress in daily life hold riotous, and sometimes terrifying, carnival.

Some of the male writers I have met and talked to over the years do not want to write about this inner world. To them, it's not a masculine province but a feminine one. These are writers who cling to a rigid division between inner and outer worlds, and value only the outer one. The inner one is taboo. Feelings, etcetera, can only be written about when projected, often unconsciously, outside. Then apparently real characters can act in a real world. These writers don't go in for this psychologising, self-indulgent stuff. Similarly, they don't read many books by women, feeling suspicious that they're going to be forced back inside into some messy emotional space. Masculinity, for many men in this culture, involves wrenching yourself away from identification with the female, stating your difference. So feminine things have to stay out of reach, and for many male readers the novel remains a feminine thing, a reminder of the mother who must be got away from. A reminder, perhaps, of the power the mother once wielded over the tiny boy.

Women readers and writers do not experience the problem in the same way. Men are held up to us for admiration. Though we may have power in the home, in the family, much of the power in the outer world is still associated with men, including in the literary world. The great literary canon, until recently, consisted mostly of works by men. We grew up reading the great male writers and were taught that great art was androgynous. It transcended the history which produced it and spoke about the eternal human verities. I think now that insisting that art is transcendent of gender simply allowed many men into that feminine novelistic space, as writers and readers, while at the same time it allowed women to escape the limitations of traditional femininity and become artists, the highbrow form of which was always seen as a masculine identification. The androgynous imagination, written about by Virginia Woolf and others, represented a different strategy for the different sexes. At the same time men went on having higher status as writers. Rather like women being cooks and men being chefs. People still make the distinction between writers and women writers. That's how far the concept of androgyny's got us. No wonder serious and ambitious female writers insist they are *not* women writers but *writers*. If you're the one that's gendered, you're the one that's put down. So perhaps either we should all be gendered or all not be gendered. Until the day of decision, I continue to refer to male writers when it's appropriate. Angela Carter saw the absurdity of all this. She refused to fit into the categories offered her. She was incapable of being a lady writer or an authoress, writing neat tales about feminine marital predicaments, as she was also incapable of pretending that sex and gender didn't matter when in fact they fascinated her. She embodied an identity of stroppy femaleness, out of Rabelais by Chaucer and the eighteenth-century female wits, with a good dash of panto dame humour when needed, mixed up with an identification with the scene-shifters and all those in walk-on parts, the spear-carriers and soubrettes. She's been a liberating example to those of us who've come just after her.

The best writers and the most generous readers, I'd suggest, have not androgynous but bisexual imaginations. That's to say they resist simplistic either/or categorisation in favour of saying *and*. You don't have to choose between identifying solely with masculine or feminine experience, as you don't have to deny that these words matter. You can explore both. You don't have to value the outer world at the expense of the inner one but can experience, through writing and reading, how they map themselves on to each other, transform each other. You don't have to believe in realist fiction at the expense of the unconscious life; they can fertilise each other. My image of the bisexual imagination is rooted in the memory of my parents, so different in their culture and religion and language, yet their books all tumbled together in the big bookcase and their words tangling and dancing at family mealtimes. This imagination is something very alive and active and sexy going on in the mind. Not static. Not transcendent. If I'd been braver when I was eighteen, and stuck up for the Georgette Heyer novels I read in secret, I'd have praised how, for example, she enjoyed herself, in *The Masqueraders*, letting her hero and heroine both cross-dress and enjoy each other's worlds, just as in *An Infamous Army* she both recreated the Battle of Waterloo, blow by blow, and also showed what the women were getting up to back in Brussels.

One strategy, for men who want to explore some kind of inner space, the association of creativity with memory, has been to turn to biography and memoirs. Biography is popularly supposed to be newly attractive because it tells the A–Z stories that the modern novel refuses. There's more to it than that. Biographies also allow for an ending, for death. Also, they can include all the topics many men have felt edgy about putting into novels: feelings, childhood experiences, domestic detail. These don't have to be projected elsewhere and transformed. They can be owned. Similarly, with the current spate of autobiographical writing by men. Feminism opened up a space for women to come out as women and write about it, if we wanted to (of course not everybody did) and now the men are talking back, telling us what it's like to be them. This is happening in lots of different literary forms, and it's a conversation, between readers and writers, I'm happy to be part of.

WORDS ACROSS THE WATER

Royal Society of Arts lecture broadcast on Radio 3,
15 September 1994, in the series *These Islands Now*

Wulf and Eadwacer is a poem in Old English, written ten centuries ago or so, which I've always remembered from my student days because it's spoken in such a direct and intimate voice. Out of the mists of the past comes this powerful female lament. 'Wulf is on one island,' cries the speaker: 'I on another.' Separation is the theme; exile and loss.

Often it can seem as though to be British is to be on one island, and to be European on another, with little hope of a prolonged affectionate meeting. Of course, there are complex historical, political and ideological reasons for this feeling that many British people have – that to be British is not to be European – and sometimes our island seems less cut off than at others. Sometimes the tides of wariness recede, revealing a causeway, across which visitors and pilgrims can pass, rather as Mont St Michel off the Normandy coast periodically reveals itself to be part of the mainland, its marsh and mud.

Today I'm going to look at some of the emotional reasons we may have for not rushing into Europe's embrace, with regard to literature: how we read the books that come to us from that other island across the water, those foreign novels, and how we might dissolve any obstacles standing in the way of our enjoyment, rocks and whirlpools of difficulty, perhaps, or flat calms of indifference.

Translation is the key word here. It is certainly translation which enables us in Britain to read those novels published abroad in a host of foreign – European – tongues. As far as I can tell, more foreign novels are being published here than ever before. There seem to be more prizes given for translation than ever. Similarly, translation is increasingly being viewed as a compelling branch of academic study as well as an invaluable practical resource. Foreign novels even appear, from time to time, in our bestseller lists. Yet although the translation industry appears to be thriving, I get the impression, at the same time, that we're not, in the mass, we British, awfully keen on reading the works produced. Our word 'foreign' doesn't help, with its connotations of strange, weird, hard to know, difficult to make sense of. While in mainland Europe ancient traditions still persist of treating visiting foreigners as guests to be welcomed and given hospitality (though this is being dented in the current political climate) here in Britain we're often suspicious of strangers. We can be unfriendly, even hostile.

This is spelt out clearly in pre-war novels, particularly thrillers, thrillers being the literary form where we most obviously display our fears, anxieties and desires. Since a major, though unstated, aim of early Agatha Christie novels, for example, seems to be to fend off worries about the breakdown of the class system and the security it afforded to the home-owning, servant-employing upper middle classes, the books are peopled with honourable, upstanding British heroes evincing a stiff-upper-lipped distaste for those born beyond the pale. In this country house world, foreigners are easily recognised, with their swarthy skins, pronounced features, funny accents and grammar, and villainous propensities. In the anxious world of the thriller, in which all is not what it seems, mirroring the way that society at large was threatening to collapse as war loomed, the foreigner becomes the scapegoat, rather as the devil did in earlier times. And because Agatha Christie so cleverly uses a small, fat Belgian as her mouthpiece, she can get away with saying the most outrageous things.

Yet Britain is changing, and with it our sense of foreignness. The pre-war version of Us and Them has shifted, and for some of us it has almost completely melted away. Nowadays, in a post-war post-colonial world of complex migrations and settlements, to be British can mean being a white person choosing to move to Canada, to South Africa, to Australia, as it can also mean to be a third-generation black citizen of London or Birmingham. We've become a multi-cultural society which has thrown up a host of writers exploring that phenomenon, with a little more subtlety, perhaps, than was available to Agatha Christie; and the English novel, the thriller very much included, has become renewed and reinvigorated in that process. English remains our common tongue, an English enriched and enlivened by the new words coming into it, as has always been the case. So we're redefining Britishness; our sense of Britishness is expanding, becoming more inclusive and more generous. To be British has, after all, always meant to be a mixture: mongrels, all of us, from different pasts, places and cultures. That is our heritage, going way back, and we should be proud of it.

Can we expand *British* into also meaning *European*? One of our stumbling blocks appears to be language; our lack of knowledge of foreign languages coupled to our expectation that foreigners will have learned to speak English; our need to depend upon translations.

I've been lucky, I think, in that the circumstances of my life have meant that I've recognised the need for translation, almost from the day that I was born, as simply part of the daily business of sorting out how to live with other people. My twin sister and I, as tiny children, seem to have spoken a private language to each other, a combination of gestures, grunts, telepathy and secret words. I used to translate for my sister, who talked later than I did, when it was necessary to address the grown-ups, and then I would translate back again from them to her. I was bilingual, with a French mother and an English father, and grew up hearing those two languages behave like lassos thrown across the dining-room table over supper, tangling and twisting, knotting and unknotting, flying loose again, as my young parents translated themselves to each other, feelings into words. My mother, like many immigrants at that time, felt, I think, that in order to survive she must assimilate completely into the dominant English culture, speak perfect English, adopt English ways and customs. Yet we children were always enchanted when at certain tense or stressful moments in family life she translated her emotional self to us: her French accent reasserted itself and she spoke with flashing eyes as a Frenchwoman. At other times, of course, we wanted her not to be different, to appear at the convent-school prize day, for example, disguised as a lady straight out of Agatha Christie, all tweeds and pearls and correctly expressed sentiments. My mother, I'm glad to say, resisted caricature, as she resisted cliché. She gave me an awareness of two cultures and two languages, of my European background, just as my father gave me the realisation of not only how the British could love the French, but how Britishness, in his case, concealed Welshness, far back, how under the correct middle-class accent was hidden a London boyhood with working-class roots, with all the jokes, turns of speech and sayings that went with that. People from different social classes, I saw, sometimes had to translate themselves to each other, just as men and women did. Translation was going on around me all the time. An emotional business.

If English and French were the tongues of Monday to Friday, Latin, that European and international language, came into its own on Sundays. My Catholic mother brought us up in her faith, and in those days the Mass was said in Latin so that anywhere in the world it would sound the same and remind us of the global, all-embracing nature of our Church. We got used to hearing tides of Latin psalms and poetry flow over our heads without knowing what they meant, and without minding that we didn't – the sound was glorious, the chanted rhythms musical, the Mass a symphony for the human voice. A parallel text in our missals meant that we knew what was going on if we wanted to. I felt at home in the Latin because I felt at home, as a child, in Catholicism, my mother's religion, and in the fact that she taught Latin, as well as French, for a living. I relished how the three languages I heard prayers in made the one prayer sound so different: Pater noster, Our Father who art in heaven, Notre Père qui êtes au ciel. In those days, for better or worse, it was Him Up There, transcendent and all-embracing and overarching, a sort of rainbow, who held all the different languages together, translated into some kind of wordless weave. Nowadays, as I'm going to suggest in a moment, I look less up to the sky when I'm searching for meaning, and more down into the waters, those cold and often stormy waters of the Channel that seem to separate us so definitively from the Continent.

I was encouraged to cross those waters, and here again I was fortunate, by my education. I read English Literature, a privilege in those days of grants; a privilege again since my parents were able to save to pay their share of the grant; a privilege to learn, as was heartily dinned into us, that our literature is written in a European language, saturated in words from our Germanic past, soaked in words from Latin and French. To read English Literature we had to tackle the European languages. To read Milton we had to take on Virgil. We read *Paradise Lost* alongside the *Aeneid* – with, in my case, much help from a crib. To read the epic of *Beowulf* in Old English, we had to learn about the Icelandic sagas, the existence of languages like Old High German, the fact that Anglo-Saxon poets referred as easily to stories from the Bible and patristic texts in Latin as to an oral tradition, linking us to Scandinavia, that circulated in the vernacular. To read medieval English religious and love poetry I had to look at the poets of northern France, the troubadours of Provence, the Celtic motifs that popped up in Cornwall, as in Brittany, as in Wales. Poets and saints of both sexes, the keepers and writers of literature, were always travelling; life on this earth meant exile from God and heaven, so you jumped into a coracle, if you were Irish, and made for Northumbria, to bring new learning and truth to those heathen English, or you wrote poems about sailing to paradise and finding magical islands where beasts could talk and the stones could sing. A wandering béguine like Mechtild of Magdeburg, who wrote down her radical, subservive mystical visions in thirteenth-century Germany, turns up in a Middle English manuscript version in the Bodleian. And so on. Oxford in those days was often classbound, stuffy and misogynist, but it gave me a powerful sense of what we now call comparative literature, how European literatures web and weave together and feed each other.

Then, in the late sixties, those of us growing up as rebels also turned to Europe for inspiration. Not only to America. We had books on existentialism sticking out of our coat pockets. We read, in translation, the novels of Sartre, Camus, de Beauvoir, the works of the surrealists and the situationists, the poets like Eluard and Aragon, and a little later some of us went on to devour, in translation of course, de Beauvoir's *The Second Sex.* French books were our gateway to Europe. They were very much what we thought of as important at the time.

We were reading from desire. That was the impetus that sent us rushing to those books, rushing through them, talking to each other about them. That's the only way to read a book, because you passionately want to, passionately need to, not because you dully feel you ought to. And perhaps there can all too often be a feeling of duty about reading European literature: I really ought to keep abreast of developments, I really ought to know more than I do about what's happening with the European novel, now that we're becoming part of Europe I really must get down to reading some European novels.

It all sounds like a tremendous amount of hard work, to be put off for another time, when one is feeling more self-disciplined. Underneath all these dutiful feelings lurks another: I shan't enjoy that sort of reading, I shan't get the pleasure I seek in reading, the reassuring pleasure of a recognisable world, European books will be too difficult to get into, after a hard day at work I need something I can curl up with and relax into – if I'm going to read a book at all. Words themselves seem to get in the way: we allow ourselves to consume Italian fashion, for example, Italian industrial and domestic design, Italian food, Italian art and Italian opera, but we're not quite so keen on Italian literature. Calvino is now widely read here, and Sciascia to a lesser extent, Natalia Ginsburg also, Umberto Eco perhaps, but few of us read any of the younger writers. Which is of course our loss.

Why does Europe, in this sense, still feel so far away? Why does it feel so hard, so difficult, so time-consuming, to transport our imaginations there through the pages of a book?

Part of the problem is that we're stuck on our island, surrounded by water. We need to find a way across.

Translation literally refers to finding that way across. The word 'translation' comes from the Latin *trans*, across, and *latum*, from the supine of the verb *ferre* to carry: a translation, a carrying across.

One of the earliest ways of crossing the water surrounding our island was by boat. By ferry. Where are we crossing to? What destination awaits us?

European literature provides us with a potent image of a boatman ferrying frightened people across a cold, dark stretch of river: Charon taking the souls of the dead across the river Styx, the entrance to the underworld. Dante takes the classical image from Virgil's *Aeneid* and reshapes it. Dante stands, in his persona as pilgrim as well as poet, next to his poet-guide Virgil, watching as the queue waiting to get on the ferry finally wakes up to what's in store – and I quote from Mark Musa's translation from Penguin Classics:

> *all those souls there, naked, in despair,*
> *changed colour and their teeth began to chatter*
> *at the sound of his announcement of their doom.*
> *They were cursing God, cursing their own parents,*
> *the human race, the time, the place, the seed*
> *of their beginning, and their day of birth.*
>
> *Then all together, weeping bitterly,*
> *they packed themselves along the wicked shore . . .*
>
> *Charon, with eyes of glowing coals,*
> *summons them all together with a signal,*
> *and with an oar he strikes the laggard sinner . . .*
>
> *so did the evil seed of Adam's Fall*
> *drop from that shore to the boat, one at a time,*
> *at the signal . . .*
>
> *Away they go, across the darkened waters,*
> *and before they reach the other side to land*
> *a new throng starts collecting on this side.*

Does the thought of reading a translation, venturing into the unknown, call up deep, unconscious images of being taken across dark waters to a place we dread; the finality of death? Fear of dying, after all, runs so deep in many of us that we don't ever acknowledge it at all, laugh at the very idea, pooh-pooh suggestions such as this one as absurd, fantastic.

If those dark, cold waters heaving under the boat don't represent the movement towards death itself, then perhaps they represent the passage down towards something else we might fear: the unconscious, that deep subterranean or underwater kingdom peopled with monsters and fairies, with ghosts and mermaids. Out of our element, we fear to drown.

So for the voyage to Europe, it might be time to abandon the laborious method of transport, the coracle; the time-honoured one, the ferry; and choose the newest one: the Channel Tunnel. Nineteenth-century British cartoons of the proposed tunnel showed it precisely as the gaping mouth to hell, on occasion a mouth transformed into the devouring *vagina dentata* of the deepest male insecurities. But *we* need have no such fears: we leap aboard our train and dive beneath the waters; we let the sea close above our heads.

Water, in all the folk tales and fairy stories of Europe, is the place which allows us to become fluid and to dissolve. It's the in-between place, the crossing-over place, like dusk or dawn; it's the place of transitions and transformations. It's the place of imagination, of memory, the place where we've buried all the feelings and experiences we can't bear to remember, all the desires and anxieties we want to forget. Nosing towards Europe in our magical underwater train, who knows what we'll encounter from the past? Who knows what the future might hold?

We might be frightened of making this journey, of allowing this translation to take place, if we've allowed Europe to become the repository for things in ourselves we feel uncomfortable about. Think, for example, of the way that the late eighteenth-century

English Gothic novels were so often set in Italy, Spain, Germany, in dramatic landscapes of castles and crags whose wildness provided the perfect setting for the perils and pitfalls confronting the heroine. Forbidden sex, adulterous sex, violent sex, incestuous sex, the very stuff of the Gothic novel: these longings and terrors of the British human heart had to be placed *elsewhere*. A happy ending meant rescue from the lures and wiles of Europe. The early Victorian novel played the same tune: think of Charlotte Brontë's vilification of the Continent, in *Jane Eyre* and *Villette*, as the home of all that's tawdry, immoral, amoral, dirty – and perhaps deeply desired even as it's shunned.

So fear of translation might represent a kind of agoraphobia, where the fear of the journey outwards covers over the fear of what we'll encounter *inside*: our turbulent adolescent selves, our unruly childish selves, those incestuous wishes towards our parents that we have had to repress and disown, those secret longings to experiment with forbidden or perverse forms of sex, those fantasies of cruelty and revenge, those *temptations*; everything we're supposed to give up, in short, in order to turn into nice, kind, hardworking, reasonable adults wearing clean clothes and living in hygienic houses. The dark stranger can go on lurking over the water in Europe, that suitably dark place, so that we won't have to find out that his is a face all too familiar to us; his is a name we know all too well.

Too absurd, you cry. Dislike of reading foreign books equivalent to fearing death and our repressed wishes for forbidden sex? What ridiculous nonsense.

At this point, some of you may be wishing that you had taken the plane, that you had already arrived and were at this very moment relaxing in a hotel whose smoothly international design assuages any anxieties about having come so far.

Too late. You've been with me so far, and so here we are, still under the waters of the Channel, deep down under the sea – and all we have to do, of course, is: enjoy it. Having plunged so bravely into our fears, what we discover next are the pleasures of this method of travelling, the ease and speed with which we are catapulted – translated – out of Britain and into Europe.

During our crossing, we're immersed in water, the fluidity of language. On the Channel Tunnel train itself, language changes over halfway. The announcements, which have been made first in English and then in French, by a *chef de bord* who speaks both perfectly, are now made first in French and then in English. So we know we've crossed over.

And what we find *down under* the water is another kind of language, the play of the unconscious imagination, which works as poetry does, as dreams do, through free-association, through metaphor.

Metaphor can change one thing into another in the twinkling of an eye. Metaphor effects magical transformations. In dreams, in poems, we can open a door in a London street and find ourselves inside a café in Venice, or we can stride up a hill in Surrey and find the palaces of Granada. Metaphor puts one thing close to another, collapses the distance in between, lets one thing become another. 'Metaphor' comes from the Greek for removal. A removals van in modern Greece will have METAPHOR written on its side. As a translation, that van is winged, goes at the speed of thought, of fantasy, of desire.

Translation depends, therefore, upon our imaginations, which are very powerful and rapid and enable us to be whisked away, rapt away, translated – like the relics of saints in medieval Europe which were regularly stolen and ferried from one church to another to give the latter greater repute. In reading, in being translated, we have to lie back and allow ourselves to be rapt away, stolen away – another of those forbidden wishes, perhaps; and perhaps, too, one recognised and indulged in more by the readers of romances than of drier texts.

It's not our willpower that's the issue in reading novels in translation, therefore. It's not our sense of duty. It's our *desire*: to let ourselves go and be carried away. Reading a translation comes to mean accepting our sexual desires, our sexual curiosity, our sexual fantasies. Owning these as part of ourselves, rescuing them back and bringing them home, we release in ourselves tremendous energy for reading, for exploring, for finding out, for going abroad and making new discoveries.

And what do we find? That swimming in the waters of the imagination, of the unconscious, together in the same place, we are alike, all in the same element, able to dissolve our differences and recognise our common humanity, these human wishes, desires, fears, longings, impulses, anxieties.

So the water becomes not only the stretch of Channel that guards and protects us from invasion from outside, not only that which separates us from Europe; it becomes that which joins us together, which brings us together and holds us together; it is a stream flowing through Europe, not a dividing sea.

The waters of the imagination transform us and our emotional geography, so that she who was a stranger becomes a neighbour and what was foreign becomes the place where we are most truly at home.

Our homeland is the imagination, also called Britain, also called Europe; the land under the sea full of secrets, slippery with darting and dancing words.

THE MYSTERY OF THE MAN IN BLACK

Children's Literature in Education, vol. 28, no.1, 1997

I had always wanted to re-read *The Black Riders* by Violet Needham, for, although I could remember very little of the story, I was aware that I had found it powerful and exciting and that it had stirred me deeply, though I no longer knew why, if I ever did. When I recalled the book, I saw a swirl of black and felt something thrilling, which to my childish mind had seemed, I was sure, adult and sophisticated, unknown and dangerous. I got the book out of the local children's library. I think I was ten or eleven at the time, more or less the same age as Dick, the hero.

The story is set in an invented European country, exotic enough to be ruled by an emperor and teeter on the brink of revolution, cosy enough to evoke the reader's own familiar landscape of home. The landscape holds rivers and forests and cliffs, villages and castles, ancient cities and proud citadels. Austria crossed with Devon, perhaps. At any rate, the foreignness of the setting permits and entices the reader into a fantasy world which feels extremely real, both modern and timeless. Transport is by horse and caravan, or fast car, or barge. Goatherds potter in the meadows while the elite crack corps, the Black Riders of the book's title, patrol the land searching for conspirators and traitors and striking terror into everyone's hearts.

Dick gets caught up in the plotting by accident at first, then chooses to risk prison and punishment by helping the rebels led by the man known as Far-Away Moses. Opposing Far-Away, and upholding his own version of law and order, is Count Jasper the Terrible, chief of the Black Riders, boss of the Citadel, and finally Regent of the troubled kingdom. He is tall, dark and handsome, courageous and austere, steely and ruthless, with a troubled past; a widower with a small daughter, Judith, who adores Dick as soon as she meets him. Dick, after many adventures, chases and escapes, can no longer help Far-Away and his band of Confederates, for he is captured, finally, by the Black Riders, and imprisoned in the Citadel, where Far-Away Moses also ends up. Caught up in the drama is the young and beautiful aristocrat Wych Hazel, who at one stage hides Dick and Far-Away in her house, which is then searched by Count Jasper and his men. They find the secret door in the panelling, the turret room, and the subterranean passage by which the boy and his mentor have fled, and Jasper warns Wych Hazel of the dangers she is running in aiding the enemies of the state. The book ends with the death of the Emperor, Jasper as Regent, Far-Away reprieved and recognised as both heroic and good, Judith and Dick fast friends, Dick's true parentage revealed, and Jasper and Wych Hazel both nursing secret dreams.

The book is certainly a rattling good story for that child I was, avid reader, tomboy, would-be writer, daydreamer, fantasy-spinner. Dick as protagonist was fun to identify with. The story was colourful and swift-paced, with lots of action, suspense and surprise twists. Re-reading it almost forty years later, it was easy and enjoyable to analyse why I had so loved it. I also, however, received the most tremendous shock. More of that in a minute.

The story constitutes a particular powerful version of a family romance, that is, it deals with the emotions, fears, longings and desires a child has about parents, growing up, puberty and sex. At the same time as it raises anxieties, it calms them. While it points to problems, it solves them. While it points to what is repressed, it performs the work of repression. So the story also functions as a kind of pattern book for parents and children. It deals with these questions: what is a good father? what is a good son? It's about men and masculinity. Mothers and daughters don't feature. Dick is that magical and classic creature out of fairy tale: an orphan, a foundling, brought up by an uncle and aunt who foster him, who feels all alone in the world until he confronts his destiny and finds a family in which he can truly belong. Not an ordinary family but a glamorous one. That's the point.

Now, when I read Dick's story in *The Black Riders*, I track how he and Count Jasper both are being taught how to be good men. Far-Away Moses is crucial to both quests. He is idealised, like a saint. He is gentle, loyal, unflinchingly brave, truthful, wise, kind, far-seeing. He is your perfect English gent of *circa* 1939 (when the book was first published) but besides being a model of upper-crust perfection he is *also* a radical dedicated to fighting despotism and injustice. In terms of the family romance enacted by the book, he is the Good Father *par excellence*. He teaches Dick how to be a man, and he also softens and sweetens the terrible Jasper, his former beloved friend until they find themselves fighting on opposite sides. By the end of the book they are friends and brothers once more. Jasper, I am afraid, stands as the Bad Father. To Dick, and his other countrymen, at any rate. He is strict and punitive, all too prone to sentencing people to death and calling for the firing squad at dawn. It's interesting to see how, in the course of the tale, the child's tendency to split Good Father so drastically from Bad Father (I mean the reader as child) gets modified. Far-Away becomes less of a total hero, in that he gives up rebelling, accepts reality, and consents not to meddle with Jasper's government, while Jasper learns to admit his tenderness and capacity to love and develops the virtues of compassion and mercy. The female characters are rather like angels, providing succour and shelter when needed, and serving to remind Jasper, particularly, of his feeling, vulnerable side. All pretty conventional, which is of course why, aged ten or so, I loved it so much. I could identify with Judith, Jasper's daughter, the wilful, brave and passionate eight-year-old who saves Dick's life, who is strong and beautiful and feminine, the only really attractive female character in the book, and I could hope to identify with Wych Hazel, who embodied for me a kind of femininity I was rather scared of: sweet, pretty, easily terrified, not very good at adventures, all too prone to give the game away too soon. The brief romantic scenes between Jasper and Wych Hazel provided the Mills & Boon element in the book, his power and ruthlessness pitted against her helplessness and niceness. I'm afraid she comes across as a bit dim-witted, and I realised that Count Jasper thought so too but didn't mind a bit. By the end of the book, the reader knows that Jasper and Wych Hazel are in love and will marry. Jasper has proved himself at last a good father to Judith and a good surrogate father to Dick. The laws of family romance require that Judith acquire a Good Mother, and Wych Hazel fills the role admirably. So family life is tested, re-forged, reinvented, and this ideal family, with pots of money, based around a strong, charismatic father, will last for ever.

I did wonder, reading the story this time around, whether *The Black Riders* doesn't refer, in some ways, to the drama of masculinity and fatherhood played out by and underpinning the Fascism flourishing in Europe in the thirties? Jasper, striding about in his black uniform and gleaming riding-boots, accoutred with silver spurs, whip and phallic motor, is a figure of patriarchal power intended to be fascinating because of his authority. Some, at least, of his charisma derives from the potential punishments he can dish out. Wych Hazel quivers in front of him, and there are scenes between him and Dick that are charged with homoerotic feeling. Deeply repressed, of course.

What shocked me when I re-read this novel forty years on was the realisation of how sexy I had found it. The ten-year-old's sexual response leapt out at me from the story, like a flower pressed between the pages suddenly come back to life and blooming again. It was as though the book held my response, had contained it all this time. I felt that I'd hidden it in the book, to keep it safe. Now there it was, waving and shining. I felt very close to that ten-year-old girl I'd been. What else could I have done with sexy feelings, at the age of ten, but hide them? I could never have openly expressed them in my family, for Catholicism taught that children did not have sexual feelings and that you only had sexual feelings once you got married. Having sexy thoughts was very wicked, such a terrible sin it could never be mentioned. So *The Black Riders* both turned me on and made me feel guilty. Secret pleasure reading it; secret guilt. Count Jasper represented my father, with whom I was in love. I didn't know this was normal for little girls. I couldn't admit it to myself, because it was too terrible and frightening. So I lived it out in fantasy by plunging into the love scenes between Jasper and Wych Hazel.

I read *The Black Riders* just after reaching puberty, when I was in the throes of guilt-laden passion for my father. I re-read it nearly forty years later when I was trying to put a form on all that turmoil by writing a novel called *Impossible Saints* in which an ex-Catholic woman struggles to understand whether mystical visions can co-exist with an active sex life outside marriage. Slowly and painfully I negotiated bouts of writer's block, periods of silence, dryness and near-despair. Finally I realised that it was my own ghosts and demons that I was to some extent exorcising. Finally I allowed myself to draw on my adolescent sexual desires and resulting guilt, deeply repressed and, I thought, long gone, and then, in doing so, at last found my form, something like a fairy tale, consisting of a secret biography interspersed with fairytale saints' lives. In the middle of all this struggle I re-read *The Black Riders*. It helped me remember, as it helped me see how memories are stories. Stories about myself and my father surfaced as I read the story of Jasper and Wych Hazel. At the advanced age of forty-seven I suddenly received a terrific charge of sexual and creative energy, came out to myself about how much I'd fancied my father and how guilty I'd felt, cheerfully wrote a pornographic short story making conscious what I now saw as the sub-text of *The Black Riders*, a pastiche hovering between comedy and tackiness, finished writing my novel, and at last felt able to cherish the passionate little girl I'd been at the same time as realising quite how destructive and damaging Catholicism had been for me. So I'm very grateful to Violet Needham.

ON THE SHELF: MRS GASKELL

The Sunday Times, 3 May 1995

My idea of a classic novel is one that I shan't tire of re-reading. *Wives and Daughters* by Mrs Gaskell fits this definition perfectly. I read it about once a year and discover it afresh each time. Mrs Gaskell died before she completed this masterpiece, so that the reader has to furnish the happy ending for herself. You see it coming from early on, when little Molly Gibson is comforted in her sorrow by sturdily good Roger Hamley and learns to trust and look up to him, but it's great fun, as this fat triple-decker unrolls its tale of provincial politics and intrigues, waiting for the inevitable denouement. There is so much to enjoy along the way, such acute observation of human behaviour and motives, such gleefully depicted social comedy, such riproaring descriptions of female passion and sensuality.

The narrator is that Victorian omniscient one who can see into everybody's hearts; definitely female. I call it maternal narrative, the voice Mrs Gaskell perfects in this novel, a voice expressing warmth and compassion towards all the characters, containing them within her deep knowledge of human frailties and foibles, understanding them, teasing them, occasionally upbraiding them. The central story is that of doctor's daughter Molly Gibson, who grows up motherless in the little town of Hollingford, adoring her father (a mutual passion very moving to read about) and tremendously upset when a stepmother, less classically evil than weak and foolish, arrives on the scene. Molly's struggles to deal with her jealousy and pain, her quest to grow up, to subdue her rebellious passionate heart in the interests of becoming conventionally feminine (never quite achieved, thank goodness), are sketched with sympathy and wit. But it's the entire town we get to know, all its meddling, warring factions divided by money, class and snobbery. Mrs Gaskell brilliantly re-creates this world of Whigs and Tories, crusty squires, hungry angry tenants, Amazonian spinsters, social climbers (real creepies and crawlies), tradespeople and French *émigrés.* The scene of the Charity Ball, where they're all forced to socialise, is one of the most brilliantly realised in the entire novel. On the way we take in large doses of medicine, religion, philanthropy, science, fashion: all the topics Mrs Gaskell herself was interested in.

The novel's psychology gives it a completely modern feel. Mrs Gaskell pre-dated Freud in her recognition of the power and volatility of repressed feelings, the subtle sideways fashion in which secret wishes express themselves and act themselves out. The word 'unconscious' peppers her plot. Freud himself remarked that writers had penetrated the secrets of the human heart long before he did. Mrs Gaskell's novels are proof of that. She understood femininity acutely, because she did not repudiate it, was immersed in it, saw its shortcomings, recognised how as a social code it boiled down to little more than hypocritical observation of male-defined etiquette. Molly is painted as an idealised portrait of what femininity *could* be: loyal, loving, intelligent, long-suffering, potentially maternal, principled, honest. Molly's saved from plaster-sainthood by her 'faults': she sits in the cherry tree to read books, she hates formal visiting and manners, she loves solitary walks, she has odd friends, she has a passionate temper and is much given to rushing upstairs for a good cry when thwarted. Much of the book's painful comedy derives from Molly's clashes with her stepmother, for Mrs Gibson (a masterpiece of a character) represents the negative side of Victorian femininity in the middle classes: she traps her husband into marriage, is a bad mother, behaves deviously and tyrannically at home, yet affects total unconsciousness of the wiles and tricks she employs to get her own way. Mrs Gibson is necessary; as anti-heroine who schemes and plots in order to survive and find economic and material security, she shows up the impossibility of the bourgeois ideals of purity and niceness. She's nice as can be, she flatters and cajoles, but it's all lies. But Mrs Gaskell doesn't blame her and we don't either; we're made to see what a tough life she's had as a widow trying to earn a living. Her daughter Cynthia is another unforgettable creation. At first she seems to do her mother credit, by epitomising all that that good lady believes young women should be: beautiful, alluring, passive, witty, accomplished at millinery, certain to marry well. But as the novel unfolds the narrator makes it clear that Cynthia has been badly brought up, separated too much from her mother as a child, exposed to bad examples and habits. She is reserved, shallow, fickle and cold-hearted. Her lovers invoke her as witch, mermaid, siren. Moralistic Mrs Gaskell shakes her head over the *bad mothering* that has brought this about. Very modern! But she's a delicious creature, not least because she breaks through all the clichés about Victorian women being represented as either angels or devils. Cynthia appears triumphantly real, complex, at times startlingly so. The relationship between these three women is the core of the book. It's fascinating to eavesdrop on all the night-time conversations in bedrooms, to see the nightcaps come off and the hair let down.

Re-reading the novel this time, I noticed the motif of open windows which runs through the text. In a book so intricately concerned with the relationships between inner life and outer behaviour, house and street, body and society, town and country, the window acts as a metaphor of connection and separation both. On the threshold of adulthood, Molly and Cynthia constantly sit by windows looking out, open windows to let in fresh air, reach through windows to catch at climbing roses, use windows as frames for their beauty. This is just one example of the clever devices of this unforgettable novel.

A NOTE ON *JANE EYRE* AS A VAMPIRE NOVEL

Jane Eyre is packed with references to the supernatural. Its Gothic, uncanny atmosphere is created by the characters themselves, from Bessie telling Jane, in childhood, spooky stories and singing her weird songs, to Mr Rochester apostrophising her, later on, as bewitching elf and fairy. Dreams, visions, forebodings and heavenly warnings all play their part, as modes of knowledge and understanding Jane can draw upon in her efforts to clear a path through confusion and work out just what is going on at night in the third storey.

Recently, during my annual re-reading of this, perhaps my favourite novel, I picked up two explicit allusions to vampirism which I had glided serenely past before. This time, they raised a pleasant shiver along my spine.

The first mention of vampires occurs in Chapter 20. Richard Mason has unexpectedly arrived at Thornfield Hall while a house party is in full swing. All the guests are roused in the middle of the night by hideous screams emanating from the attic floor – from a room just above Jane's. Rochester calms the guests, insists the noise was just a servant's nightmare, and sends everyone back to bed. Jane, however, accompanies him upstairs to the fateful room where Mason lies mauled and bleeding, having been attacked by

The Thing. Later that night, when the doctor has at last arrived, Rochester urges him to

> 'hurry! – hurry! The sun will soon rise, and I must have him off.'
>
> 'Directly, sir; the shoulder is just bandaged. I must look to this other wound in the arm: she has had her teeth here too, I think.'
>
> 'She sucked the blood: she said she'd drain my heart,' said Mason.

These are the only words in the entire novel that the unfortunate Mrs Rochester is reported as saying. The only language she produces points to herself as one of the undead. Rochester picks up the allusion when he replies to Mason: '"when you get back to Spanish Town, you may think of her as dead and buried"'.

By now the reader knows that the ghoulish visitor will refuse to lie down, will rise again, will not be buried for long in anyone's unconscious. Mason says to Rochester: '"Impossible to forget this night!"' Jane too, is unable to forget what she has heard and seen, and falls to having strange dreams as a way of trying to explain these terrifying events to herself.

It is not a dream, she is convinced, when on the eve of her wedding to Rochester, a hideous apparition enters her room, looms over her, and tears her wedding veil in two. Describing her visitor to Rochester the following day, she says it reminded her '"of the foul German spectre – the vampire"'.

Now, these references to vampires may be casual images, tossed in by Charlotte Brontë to thicken up an already seething brew. They just help beat up the Gothic atmosphere a little more, perhaps. What's a vampire or two compared with the eldritch cast of ghouls and monsters slinking in and out of this novel's overheated prose?

But the images in *Jane Eyre* don't work like that. As many readings have shown, they operate within a tight structure of linked meanings to create a webbed set of comments and suggestions running underneath the surface of the story. Images to do with colour work in this way; so do the images clustering around the themes of orphan–homeless-child–parent–home; or the images, already mentioned, to do with elves, fairies and goblins. The deepest reality of the novel is in its layers of metaphor.

Vampires, according to the essay by Ernest Jones (Freud's biographer) which I read quite recently, function as carriers of our anxieties about our Oedipal wishes and their forbidden objects, our parents. The vampire seems to stand both for the desire and for its dreaded punishment. Either you find this kind of interpretation interesting or you don't, I suppose. If you *do* accept that what we're most frightened of is simultaneously that which we most desire, then an extra *frisson* creeps into the reading of *Jane Eyre*. Various critics have pointed out that the story's pivot – Rochester not being free to marry Jane because he has a wife already – is similar to that around which Charlotte Brontë's own life was turning in anguish: she could not dream of marrying Monsieur Héger, her professor in Brussels, because he had a wife already, who was only too much alive and too anxious to drive off potential usurpers; at any rate, that's how Charlotte seems to have experienced her. The mention of vampires, in this context of forbidden love, does add an extra layer of delightful terror, terrible delight, to our heroine's predicament. Rochester, the 'master', the father-figure, may also carry echoes of early love, early desires, that must be repressed. He is both the father who evokes the banned wishes, and the lover who later on can satisfy them. I'm not suggesting for one moment anything as banal as: Charlotte Brontë suffered from unresolved Oedipal feelings about her own father; merely wondering whether she didn't allow herself to enrich the reader's shivery pleasures by thickening her plot with nicely troubling hints of incest.

Freud said more than once that the poets and artists and novelists had plumbed the depths of the human heart long before he arrived on the scene. I love to think of him lying on the couch puffing on a cigar, devouring his copy of *Jane Eyre*, and learning all about the Oedipus complex in women.

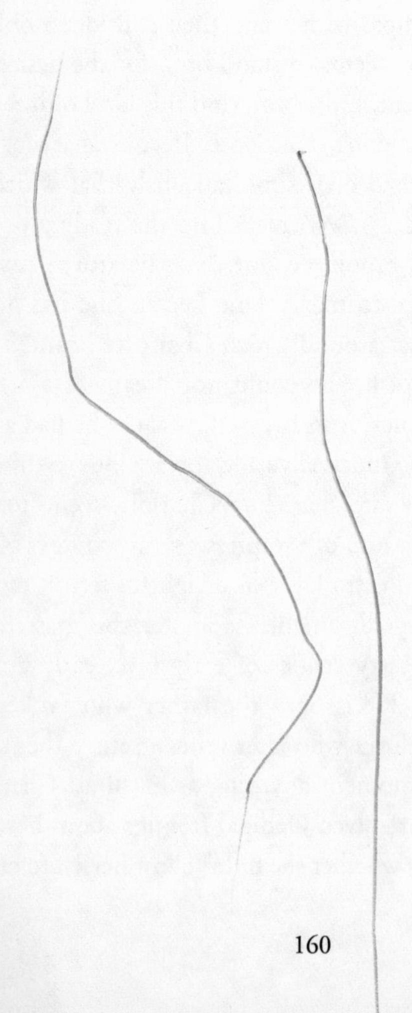

5

On Art and Artists

PISS FLOWERS

Catalogue essay for Helen Chadwick's sculpture show, 'Piss Flowers', at the Angel Gallery in Nottingham, 1995

Pearly light in the bathroom, clear flame of the cream-coloured candle, you so white in the enamel bath lolling in pale water the colour of ice. The room a box of water and sweet spices, its four sides enclosing you, just enough space for the bath, some bottles of crystals, glass jars crusted with salt, a white wrought-iron chair adrift with our clothes.

I lower myself in, on top of you. I float over you, water lapping my mouth, a mouthful of warm bathwater, I lap at you as though I'm water too, I lick and kiss you, our wet mouths full of one another in the flickering light the silky air the watery small room the deep bath that you fill my white flower open like a daisy a white gardenia whose wet cock is this whose cunt wet in the rain outside in the park under the dripping bushes drenched with sweetness in the milky dark sucking at you.

Then out of the bath, you stand me up, I stand over you leaning back on the white iron chair pressing down on layers of wet cotton, I sit on you facing you we start to laugh we spear each other, thick living flesh spike drawn into that secret mouth lips so swollen we wrestle we slide all over the place children playing in the snow tumbles of whiteness a twist of legs around crisp edges of frost we stagger and fall down.

Your skin tastes of salt and fresh sweat, it's sweet too it's milk-white your flesh, your teeth biting at me as my mouth arches around you, my tongue tests itself on you. Arms hold you to me, legs and feet plaited to ropes of white lace, a solder of wetness slips between us. Naked between coarse white sheets scratchy and smooth, a stream of moonlight like white juice down your shoulders and back over my stomach.

We are a solid white body on the white bed, melting, hard. I kneel over you, arch myself above you, pin you flat with my hands, hold you down just to tease you a little no no no go on go on. We lap at each other like cats at cream, suck and slap and tickle, I swallow you in then spit you out again, circle you with my mouth, pull you and push you, gobble you softly slowly frosty height of the white mountain icy depths of the white lake the burning stream in between. I'm your land and you're mine, you offer me everything, plenitude, emptiness, the white hollow embracing the white peak, I can have and have and have, I melt then freeze then melt again. Pleasure stalks us, a snow animal that growls and purrs, supple and fat, long slow ripples spreading out wider and wider of this new body we have made between us the body of ourselves making love arching out high up holding each other as we fall rolling over and over in the snow.

SECRET STILL LIVES: ON BONNARD

tate magazine, January 1988

She lies in the bath, while he paints. He paints her while she lies in the bath. Her thoughts are often somewhere else, so sometimes he paints her with her head out of the picture and just his slippered foot showing on the edge of the bathmat.

While he paints, he is in the studio, while she is in the bath. In the bathroom, he watches her, then goes away to the studio to paint. He dissolves her solidity into colour, into light. She lies in the bath and dissolves into a flow of images, hallucinations, snatches of words.

One way of looking at it is to see the bath as an opened oyster, sharp frilled edges prised apart by a short squat-bladed knife. Inside those stone petticoats in a swill of sea water lies the pearl. A mouth opens and closes. Soft flesh tasting of salt. The bath's claw feet curve like oyster shells, and the room swims in pearly sea colours shot through with iridescence as jewelled fishes flick past. Light scatters itself on to the floor, broken up into lozenges. Light dapples itself on to tiled walls, lino. An underwater world washed in gold, green, blue, mauve, turquoise. In other moods, at other times, pink, yellow, orange. Lying on the edge of her mind's beach, lapped by small green waves, she floats, watching blue slop between her toes. She's the prize towards which he works and which he finds at last, each time he completes a painting. Smooth, milky flesh. His lily of white enamel petals. She lies at the heart of a fiery whirl of heat as sunlight knifes its way in under the edge of the blind and sprinkles drops of gold across the floor.

If you captured a mermaid and wanted to keep her in the house, then you'd probably put her in the bathroom. Usually it's the other way round: the mermaid imprisons the man. The woman with a tail rises from the waters, entices the innocent sailor towards her with the strangeness and sweetness of her unearthly singing, the shock and charm of her nakedness, then lures him down to be lost for ever in the cold green depths below the waves. This time, the painter has captured the woman, fished her up with his bath-shaped scoop. She's on display in his aquarium, a wild creature tamed in a jar, bobbing in preservative.

Another way of looking at it is to try and imagine what she sees during those hours when she lounges, indolent as a rose-gold carp, at the bottom of the bath, her long legs stretched right out, her toes pushing her off the white wall of the far end. Chin sunk down over throat, eyes lowered, she gazes in silence, occasionally flapping her hands like fins to send rills of scented water scurrying over the clear surface of water and her skin.

Perhaps she remembers the fairy story she was told as a child, of the monster-goddess Melusine, the woman who was also a tailed creature like a great fish, the fairy creator who brought magical worlds into being on condition that her husband never spied on her while she lay in her bath. When he disobeyed, and spied on her through the keyhole, and saw her thrashing tail, and discovered the powerful monster that she was when not disguised in human form, she cried out and rose into the air and flew away and was never seen again.

The house contains the bathroom. The bathroom contains the bath. The bath contains the woman. The woman contains all kinds of meditations, memories, daydreams. Egg within egg within egg. Her husband, who loves her, paints her waiting for something. Perhaps for the pain to stop. Sometimes her thoughts scratch at her so much that only the water's caress will do, licking at her like the tips of brushes. The water paints her all over with peace. It's a treat, this bathing, and perhaps a form of treatment too. To be held in the water's arms. To forget herself, go out of herself, merge with the cool water and the hot light.

The bathroom is very well dressed. Around the naked, stooping woman are soft hills of towels, falls of curtains, a chair draped with chintz covers, her abandoned dressing-gown flung on top, a shimmering pattern of rose, dusty pink, like a heap of geraniums. Light glows inside her and outside, apricot, amber, orange, gold. Now that she's out of the bath and standing up the shapes are different: rectangles. The floor dances across and back, orange to blue and green, and the little cabinet rears up behind the bath. The frame of the tall window is firm and implacable, the louvred shutter letting in layers of pale heat. From her enclosed, interior world, in which glass bottles collect up the light, she is being summoned out. So she pulls on her self, rippling it up like an elastic belt, holding her in. Her skin, pink and shiny after her bath, is so tight and silky on her legs it looks like stockings. Tenderly her husband dresses her in flesh.

Kitchens can be like cathedrals. The yeast rises, and the panelling of the cupboards in blue-green, blue-mauve stripes, and the fluted curves of the radiator. Everything goes up: the steam of cooking, the scent of vanilla and lemon and sugar, the glossy black neck of the bottle of red wine, the eddies in the pattern of the carpet like water lapping at cathedral steps, reflections in a blood-red lagoon. Her red island in the middle is the table. She rolls her pastry out. She is the architect of cakes and tarts. She crimps and nips her dough, lets her finger and thumb pinch the edges, pierce chimneys for steam. Then she brushes her brioche palaces with beaten egg and shoves them into the oven. A man watching can see this as a kind of sacrament, because he doesn't do it himself. For her, it's daily and necessary. It's what has to be done. Painstakingly repeated over and over, to get it right. Here's the eternal present of housework and cooking. He catches it in paint, swimmy and grand as a Venetian palazzo. There she is, far below, head down as usual.

The cupboard is the house within the house. It's the hinge between outside and inside. It connects looking both ways, and it leads to a secret space that, being hidden and concealed, belongs neither to inner nor outer world. It partakes of both. It's her containing space, as the bath is too. She keeps her things in here. It's she who opens the door and takes them out or puts them away. The cupboard is an interior cave of making. Its walls are coloured red as blood. A miniature storeroom, it holds apples and grapes, bread and cheese, plates and glasses, decanters and cups. It mixes up the usual categories of keeping things separate. A larder, a treasure-trove. The kind of place that makes children want to break in and steal the riches of their mother. Men have garden sheds or studios and women have cupboards. She keeps the knives polished and sharp. Nothing in here is cracked or chipped. The apples sit in scarlet rows and the glasses sparkle. He paints an intimate portrait of what he believes his wife is like inside: red and sweet and good. She knows that red can mean angry too, the sudden desire to sweep everything off the shelves on to the floor, the urge to destroy, the desperate need to escape from the house and from him. It's a need which arrives regularly, with a rhythm she recognises. She breathes a sigh of relief. She has emptied herself of red yells, red words. The cupboard holds her silence. She can sit and look at it and take her time deciding what to put back, what to mend, what to throw away, how to arrange everything. She'll make the cupboard beautiful again, for the next time he wants to paint it. A still life in French is a *nature morte*. This cupboard has a mouth that can swing open and shut, which can answer back. It's deeply alive. Inside her live all the things she loves, all the people, animals, plants, possessions. She arranges and rearranges their images in her red memory. They change position often and dance about. She is transparent. He gazes into her and paints what he sees. Hot and red she glows like an oven and cooks up fiery dreams.

She eats little, because she is afraid of growing fat. Women must not be fat. They must be slender. Oh, she knows why. It's a secret between women, that they share, mother to daughter without words. You mustn't be bigger than a man. You mustn't remind him of when he was a little baby, powerless and needy, dependent on a woman to pick him up and feed him. If you're big, you're like the huge, powerful mother, who picked him up and dandled him and swung him about at whim, who could caress or smack him, feed or deprive him, help him or hurt him. She had that choice and that power. Now that he's grown up, a man, he's supposed to be the powerful one, a sort of god, and so you mustn't remind him that once he wasn't. Her husband is a small, delicate-looking man, who wouldn't harm a flea, and she mustn't be bigger than he is. So she starves herself gently, every day. She deprives herself of taking more than she thinks she should.

She feeds others. She gives to others. To friends and relatives, to the guests who arrive. Her own gross flesh, her potential for it, is shut away, and her slenderness is a gift to him, which helps inspire him to paint. When he paints her nude, she remains mysterious, belonging to herself. You have to listen hard to imagine what she might say. Often she poses for him indoors. Is the outdoors too bright, too enticing, too hot? What would happen to her if she wandered out of the garden on to the hillside or down into the town? Might she enjoy herself too much? Perhaps. So she draws lines of definition around herself. She creates boundaries she must not cross. She hovers on one side of the table, by window-sills, in the frames of doors.

She collects up the plenty of the garden and brings fruit and vegetables indoors. She arranges pyramids of peaches and grapes, puts redcurrants and blackcurrants in a bowl. Nothing lasts long in this climate. Produce wilts all too soon, shows the subtle bloom and fur of mould. So they must eat up what is there. She makes marvellous meals, taking great pleasure in getting others to eat. The fruit goes into tarts and pancakes, soufflés and mousses, cakes and pies. Anything over she preserves in jars which she keeps in cupboards in the back kitchen, in the cool dark. She bottles cherries in *eau-de-vie*, and greengages and plums. She makes compote of pears and apricots. She spreads feasts for others, and urges them to eat. She herself likes a cup of herbal tea, or a sip of coffee, sugarless and black.

Outside prowls the garden like an animal, proud and wild, splendid and unafraid. It pours itself up to the window and beats against the pane. She hovers inside, keeping an eye on it.

Perhaps she's afraid of too much colour, too many colours too much heat. Why? She's afraid of chaos, of mess, of her own greediness, of her own wild uncontrolled body, her own voice crying out with pleasure, pain, rage. All those things she gives to her husband. They belong to him, not to her. She appreciates them inside the frame of his pictures. She can envy them safely because he knows how to control the paint. It won't leap out and bite her. He makes it seem tame, so skilled is he, like a leopard padding quietly through the garden.

She becomes part of his painting. Head down and face averted, on the edge of things. She dissolves into schemes of colour, arrangements of shapes. She's pleased. She lets go into this embrace. She's a small part of the painting, and all that is inside her is spread around her, like the symbols in a dream, for the viewer to read.

He loves his wife and so he learns to see through her eyes as well as his own. He notices the things that she does: the hang of a tablecloth, the gesture of hands flopping circles of pastry on to pie tins, how an apple sits on a plate waiting to be peeled. He records what some dismiss as bourgeois pleasures: the calm progress of domestic life. To be pigeonholed, if not despised.

That's not quite it, as they both know, though they don't talk about it. In fact the hint of her unease, of her occasional troubled darkness, gives the paintings their necessary edge, undertow, shadow, sharpness. Perhaps these qualities belong in him too. Perhaps he's given them to his wife, in exchange for the passion and colour she gave him. Perhaps a marriage sometimes involves this flow and exchange of gifts. Together they make a complete creature, who suffers as well as loves, who both sulks and laughs. Both of them do this. Only convention fixes them into woman and man. Is that true? Both of them are artists, she in the house and he in the studio. Is that true? They need and sustain each other. His paintings celebrate what she brings to his life. She can't tell us what she thinks. He lets us imagine it.

He paints a double layer of vision. What he sees, and what he might see. The way things are when you really can look and really can see. To say he paints a transfigured world sounds as though he's inventing it, glossing it, making it false. No. He paints the reality. It's just that most of us can't bear to look at it most of the time. Or else we simply can't see it when we look.

He paints the world as paradise. Not sweetened or sugared up, idealised or sentimentalised. This paradise is around us all the time, if only we could let ourselves see it.

To see it, you have to see whole.

Paradise is lost. Paradise lost. We grow up, and learn to classify, to separate, to divide. We are divided, inside ourselves and between ourselves. Man and woman, inside and outside, human being and natural world, the garden and the house.

Children see whole, before they're torn out of paradise and grow up.

He paints what has been lost and now found again. He paints its restoration. He paints what's missing and what's complete. He paints the garden flowing into the house through the window, the house full of the garden, its flowers and vegetables and fruits, he paints the connection of the house and the garden, their interconnection and integration. He paints human beings as part of nature, not separate from it, part of the same body. He paints the radiant body of the world from which we were once separated and to which we can now return when we look and let go and dissolve. He paints the body of the world transfigured by the look of love which sees and connects everything. The light transforms and makes everything, and that's what he paints. He paints the process of seeing, loving, creating, the flux and dance of everything that is, inside and outside, how it keeps changing and changing us. How could one of these pictures ever be called finished? No wonder he sneaks into galleries and secretly touches them up.

He surrounds her with greediness and generosity, with fullness and aggression. He gives back to himself and her the body of the mother, its goodness, its knowledge of destructiveness, and in the teeth of death he paints his knowledge of death, the almond tree flowering in the spring. He dreams of his dead wife, restored to health and gaiety, and he leans forward as she opens her lips and begins to speak.

SEEING DIFFERENTLY: WHAT SELF-PORTRAITS MIGHT BE

Essay from *In the Looking Glass: an exhibition of contemporary self-portraits by women artists* (Lincolnshire County Council, 1996)

When she looked at herself in the mirror what did she see? With whose eyes was she looking? When she screwed up her eyes and stared at herself was it really she who was doing the looking? How could she know?

She gazed at herself in the mirror. A simple statement, you might think. A scene repeated in paintings down the ages. Woman, representing vanity and narcissism, lolls in front of the looking-glass, in love with herself and her own beauty. Frailty, thy name is woman. Mirrors flatter and seduce. It's how you recognise mermaids: they come armed with mirrors. Dangerous ladies, these, monsters from the waist down. Don't fall into their snares. The painters compliment the beauty languishing in front of her mirror, render the silk and softness of her naked flesh, but they also warn, admonish. Beauty means power. Be careful. Take beauty's clothes away; confine her to the bedroom.

Is that true? She felt it didn't apply to her, anyway. She was often anxious when she looked at herself in the mirror. She looked with the eyes of others, the eyes of judges, the eyes of potential lovers weighing her up before rejecting her. She was not beautiful. Not attractive enough. She split open her face with tiny hatchet blows of looking: eyes set too close or too far apart, nose too big, mouth too small or too wide. And so on. Her face was a problem to be dissected then corrected, glued back together into magazine perfection, reshaped and re-sculptured by paint. What she called blusher her grandmother called rouge. Images of fast women daringly applying lipstick and powder in public, brazenly making up their lips in restaurants after smudging scarlet on to white linen table napkins. Like Veronica's cloth, taking the imprint of Jesus' face after she mopped it, his sweat and blood. A portrait in blood. A self-portrait in blood? How could that be done? Was that what the lipstick-smudged napkin reminded her of? Was that why it shocked her?

Did beauty exist as a denial of other aspects of the body? The way its edges were constantly dissolving and changing as it shed flakes of skin, sweat snot piss shit blood etcetera? There was a clean self, which qualified for beauty, and there was a dirty one too, which she was not supposed to love, a baby self who ecstatically gave all of herself to her mother, rhythms of letting go of herself which later on she learned to call dirty. Parts of yourself had to be thrown away.

Inside her, many selves jostled in a dance. Sometimes they fought. Some of these selves were secret, or forgotten, or buried alive. Some she saw out of the corner of her eye. Some at night, when they surfaced in dreams. There was all of her childhood, and her adolescence, trailing behind her, to be gathered up. Who was she if not her childhood? How could she find out? How could she remember? Being an adult seemed to mean shutting down on the suffering and the pleasure of childhood, deciding to forget. She wanted to recover those lost selves, bring them in, she wanted to remember. Were memories true? Or were they stories that she invented for making sense of things, soap operas that kept changing as she grew up, that never ended?

The selves that chose to slap on makeup, the selves she feared she was, the selves she dreamed she might become, that she longed to escape into and towards, all these clamoured for attention and wanted to stop being secret. There was a self that made love, too, and a self that watched and commented ironically, and a self that lost itself and shouted out, currents and tides of passionate feeling. What about the self that loved other women, dreamed about them and desired them and fought with them? Was that self allowed, or did it have to be squashed down and not admitted to? What about the animal self, who ran silently in the darkness, lithe and swift, the hunter who could pounce and snarl, who never felt shame, who obeyed instinct, who just did what had to be done? Sometimes she was a beautiful wolf, or a bear. She might be an owl, or a buzzard floating on cushions of air.

Some of the selves were like disguises. Costumes she pulled on and posed in. Paradoxically these masks, this fancy dress, could make her feel more deeply herself. Nakedness was not necessarily truth. Or she could wear her skin like a fur coat, like a satin robe. She could turn into a boy, a man, if she chose. Was that a different self or the same? And that image of the mother, pressed on to her flesh in infancy by motherlove or the lack of it, or love and hate mixed up, did that matter? Was there a mother-self inside her who loved a daughter-self or was their relationship more complicated? Sometimes she felt that her artist-self was cherished and encouraged by her mother-self and sometimes not. Sometimes they embraced and sometimes not. There was the self that made art and wanted to offer it to the world as a gift. Was this the same as the baby-self who created with her own body and offered these creations to the mother? Did baby become artist, and did mother become world? How could you put all that into a self-portrait?

Perhaps, anyway, she was a machine. Her self was her intelligence and that was that?

She looked into the mirror, searching for the parts of herselves she couldn't see. The parts usually kept hidden. Hints of them . . . Traces . . . Something fleeting, gone, lost, that suggested itself in passing then vanished . . . A presence she guessed at, that she reinvented in its absence. She could begin with absence, with ignorance, with not-knowing. It made her feel free, not to know who or what she was, to start from there. She could make herself up. Re-make herself. Dream selves into being. Use her imagination. Map the contours of fear and desire. There was a self that did not yet exist, a body that had not yet been born. She could make it. She might call it her muse, or the body of love. Its names were infinite and various. It was up to her.

LA DOLCE VITA REVISITED

City Limits, 15 September 1987

The Vatican tried to ban it. A woman spat on Fellini at the première. Controversy was followed swiftly by international box-office and critical success, while the film was also hailed by the Left for its exposé of bourgeois decadence. Its title passed into common usage for a certain privileged lifestyle, and the surname of one of its characters (Paparazzo) was adopted to designate a whole breed of aggressive and intrusive photographers.

La Dolce Vita opened in 1960. It has not been available in this country for over fifteen years. I went to see it for the first time last week. My head was a jumble of history: memories of 1960 as a time of promise and change for some (my family had moved from the post-war council estate into a suburban detached house and I'd won a scholarship to grammar school), memories of 1972 when the film was last shown here (I was working as a librarian while living in a wild experimental libertarian commune, doing street theatre and writing for the underground press), memories of modern Italy where I've lived on and off for the last four years. I mention these details only to elucidate my response to the film: what surprised me about it, twenty-seven years on, was how it manages to convey the illusion of a precise historical moment and to recycle certain images that have been around for quite some time.

It's able to do this, perhaps, because it is structured like a dream (no clear plot or connections between scenes, a wonderful non-naturalistic use of landscapes and characters, a plethora of strange, disturbing and beautiful images) and because the main protagonist, Marcello, played by Mastroianni of the quizzically twitching eyebrows, is whirled through it vaguely trying to make sense of what he sees. It offers the viewer all the amoral pleasures of dreaming (just lie back and relax and stop worrying about politics) while it encourages you at the same time to construct your own narrative explanation of what it might all mean.

What it provides immediately, let me hasten to add, is enormous pleasure: stunning cinematography, visual and verbal jokes tumbling past each other, a switchback ride through its maker's imagination full of glorious excess, lovely women to gaze at and cheer on as they bewitch and bemuse our hapless hero. I went to watch it feeling merry and sexy (nothing like remembering the good ole sixties) and came out feeling five times more so.

The action is set in Rome, partly around the glamorous café society of the Via Veneto chock-a-block with trendy social climbers, and partly on the wastelands and building sites where post-war Rome is being expanded and reconstructed. Ancient or Renaissance Rome hardly appears: the interior of the dome of St Peter's is merely a backdrop for Anita Ekberg improbably dressed as a cardinal; catacombs have been converted into swinging nightclubs; the Trevi fountain simply offers Anita Ekberg a chance to wade through it in full evening dress, wet to her wonderful thighs. The camera swoops instead through bleak lonely modern housing estates, hideous new churches, hospitals identical with multi-storey car parks, bland apartments, anonymous streets. Rome, according to this dream of the modern, is no more glamorous than, and not much different from, Reading or Milton Keynes. Fellini's lack of romanticism, in this respect, makes us *see* the profiteering property development and speculation enabling a new class besides the aristocracy to get rich quick, even while he hints at the emotional and spiritual boredom that is a consequence.

The story covers seven days and seven nights in which Marcello, a journalist on a scandal magazine, with aspirations to become a Serious Writer, prowls the margins of the sweet life in search of sensation, the meaning of life and beautiful women. A prototype yuppie, lacking a sense of community and continuity, he doesn't really participate in what he observes; he's more of a voyeur; he likes to look but not to touch too much. Touching might mean commitment; to life and to women. The film unreels the imagination of a self-made man (his old dad's a bourgeois businessman while he's a groovy media person) checking out an array of initially delicious but ultimately disappointing women: the earthy golden-hearted prostitute; the bored heiress; the possessive maternal mistress; the sex bomb; the tough but sweet nightclub hostess; the innocent girl up from the country; the devoted wife; the spoilt playmate; and, since we're in Italy, the Madonna. Marcello, in the business of creating and selling fantasies through writing gossip, consumes each and all of them with his gaze, seeking perhaps a posh gourmet's composite figure of some ideal Real Woman. Luckily for him, this is impossible, since the women exist as firmly distinct archetypes; so he can go on sipping and tasting . . . Each of these women slips past him, or vanishes, or is misunderstood by him; his stance as mere onlooker creates both his hunger and his frustration, both his fantasies and his disillusion. Just as he's unable to respond quickly enough to the lovely heiress's declaration of love for him and so loses her, so in the last frames of the film he is unable to hear the words that the innocent country girl speaks to him.

Marcello has trouble with naming women (is a wife a boss? is a live-in lover a cleaning-woman?) and with understanding them as autonomous subjects: he tells a woman poet that hers are too good to be a woman's poems, slags off a woman painter and a woman singer, listens sympathetically to other men declaring that the femininity of 'oriental' women is consonant with their passive adoration of men (to travel is to fuck). Women seem easier for him to deal with when they're firmly approximated to nature as opposed to culture: chorus-girls dressed as lions, a drunken naked woman he smears with feathers, the sex queen cuddling a stray kitten. He's not so hot at conversation, prefers to watch a woman strip.

Marcello's paparazzi friends demonstrate the intrusiveness and sadism the camera is capable of in the service of gutter journalism; the camera becomes a metaphor for Marcello himself as he zooms about trying to keep all these unruly moving bodies in focus, control his vision that is constantly disrupted by the women actors in his fantasies walking off or shouting back at him. Later, Fellini would make *City of Women*, in which the wonderfully unregenerate Marcello character explicitly dreams a hellish paradise of beautiful amazons at a women's liberation conference who are still up to their old tricks; in this later movie (1980) our hero has achieved greater affection, greater wryness, laughs more.

In *La Dolce Vita*, by twinning his hero with the camera, Fellini not only bravely and brilliantly comes out as a man and explores masculine thinking; he's also enabled to engage in a playful and highly enjoyable investigation of how the imagination creates a vision of reality dependent on illusion and artifice. Perhaps Anita Ekberg's bosom doesn't exist when Marcello's not staring at it? From sex queen to queen of heaven: there's a marvellous long sequence in which the Virgin Mary, the most perfect woman of them all, *never appears*; and this can either mean that the inner-city children claiming to have visions of her are faking, or that they have *special* vision. In front of a million TV cameras they drive a mob of pilgrims to hysteria; twinkling little embryonic starlets . . .

It's old to see this film now, in Thatcher's Britain. The year 1960 ushered in an era in which a dream of profound political change was possible, fuelled by *desire*, in which a concept like co-operation could be applied to housing, trade union activity, sexual love. Thatcher's government has smashed that dream; consequently, at the same historical moment it's possible for hooray henries and yuppies to deride soppy sentimental hippie sixties politics while simultaneously ripping off and re-creating sixties imagery; beehives and minis are now sanitised, safe. People's memories are short; political advances can be forgotten, or sneered at when too threatening. Fellini's film (so beautiful, so tactile, all that delicious flesh, those heaving bosoms in little black dresses) could be used, I'd guess, for all sorts of nostalgic and even reactionary reasons, if that's what you want to do, just as it still works as an indictment of dishonesty and greed. It's big enough, good enough, rich enough, to survive reductive interpretations, including mine. We can choose to be in or out of the ring (circus/boxing/lions and Christians), Fellini seems to be suggesting; and if part of him is the cool spectator, certainly part of him is the wisecracking clown.

THE TUB

by Vanessa Bell

Writing on the Wall: Women Writers on Women Artists, edited by Judith Collins and Elsbeth Lindner (Weidenfeld & Nicolson, 1993)

The tub was made of silvery zinc, gleaming against the golden wood of the floor. It was as curved and round as her stomach. When not in use it hung from a nail in his studio. Today, because it was so hot, she'd decided to have her bath on the veranda, where the sunlight fought through the linen blinds and scorched her feet. She was going to give herself the pleasure of a bath in the afternoon. He was across the yard in his studio, working, but she was stuck. She thought she might as well take a bath. So she dropped her clothes on to the hot golden floor, then grasped the yellow curly mass of her hair and started to plait it.

He was a sculptor, and she was a writer. She wished she wasn't a writer. She didn't much like the book she was working on at the moment. It was too obvious. Too solid. It was a failure.

A sort of before-text and after-text, that's what she wished she could write. If she were cleaning up from him in his studio, which he'd never have allowed, she would like to collect up all the discarded bits which had been pared away with flicks of his knife, cherish them as equally valuable. The lost bits. You could see them as making a shape, the shape that surrounded the finished text, its echo, its mould. Yet they weren't usually considered interesting or meaningful. They were the parts that had been cut away, to give form to what their loss revealed, the shape emerging as the hand with the knife cut, cut, cut, and dropped them, gouged out, odd shapes, on to the floor, to lie among curls of woodshavings.

At the moment he was making studies of the female nude. In the mornings she modelled for him and in the afternoons she worked on her book.

She thought of the imagination as a place inside her, like an extra stomach, a geography of the interior to be mapped in darkness, then those scrawled notes to be brought out into the light, peered at, deciphered. At the moment she felt hollow and empty as the bath. So she filled the bath with jug after jug of warm water, tipped in a handful of scented amethyst salts, stirred them to make them dissolve into clouds of milk. She got into the bath and lay down. Usually she bathed with him. He'd help her wash the yellow bulk of her hair, pouring water over her head to rinse her well, his big hands moving very gently around the nape of her neck, lifting her hair, patting, holding.

She thought that if she were a sculptor she would cherish the mistakes. The fragments that didn't fit, that had to be thrown away for the work of art to be made, reveal itself. She thought she'd like to work with those. Pick them up, reassemble them into what might have once been their original shape, or might not, and glue them together. She'd leave the joins showing, the lines of glue, oh yes. So that you could see she'd made it up out of waste bits. She was the one who'd construct the double of the work of art, its shadow. Insubstantial. Patched up. She wanted to see them side by side. The statue. And its discarded case, mended chrysalis. She didn't know why, really. Except perhaps to show where it came from. Its origins, before it was worked on, in a block of wood. Hewn from a tree chopped down in a forest. She wanted to construct the shell of the work of art. Reconstruct it. To take a handful of litter; wood chips; and reassemble them. From an absence into a presence. What she would do with this she had no idea. Destroy it again probably. Then start afresh.

She stepped out of the bath and let the heat of the sun towel her dry. She emptied the bath. She carried jug after jug of tepid water to the edge of the veranda and flung it over the plants jostling at the garden's edge. The bath gleamed, scoured out by sunlight, silvery and golden. She loosened her hair from its tight plait pinned on top of her head, and it sprang out, a crackling mass.

Still too hot to put her clothes back on. She padded barefoot to the bedroom and put on a thin cotton kimono printed with a pattern of red and yellow flowers. She liked it because it was so old and worn that it was comfortable as her own skin. She liked the pattern, its faded colours. When it was new the red had been too bright. She'd washed it repeatedly in too-hot water to subdue it. She'd left it out in the scorching sunshine to pale a bit. Now it was just right. Very soon it would fall apart. Already it was irrecoverably torn under the arms. She poured herself a glass of red wine and sat down at her writing table. With one hand she turned over the sheets of paper in front of her on the white wood surface and with the other she absentmindedly rummaged in her yellow mane, tossed it, to turn it like meadow hay, smelling of sun, very dry.

Drops of water flew from her hair and landed on the handwritten pages of her novel. The ink puddled and swam. The words dissolved like bathsalts in the bath. They were rinsed off, streaks of blue.

She tore up these chapters she so disliked. She made a fist and let a stream of white pieces of paper, stained with blue, flow from it.

She knelt on the floor and picked them up one by one. She laid them out on the table at random and shifted them about, as though these indecipherable torn-up bits of text were part of a collage. The word *text* gave her pleasure. A sensual word. Like *pelt*: to be stroked and caressed and made to shine. To be teased out with the fingers into a mass of loose wet connected words.

She fetched the notebooks in which she had first scribbled the notes for this stuck novel. She opened them, read and re-read, sipping her wine, sitting comfortably with one leg hooked underneath her and one foot bracing her tilted body against the floor. She tore out the pages she most enjoyed reading and strewed them on the table in front of her. She tore out the phrases and words which most appealed to her. She laid them side by side in new arrangements.

She thought of him, how at night in bed their bodies pressed together, dented one another, pushed and pulled each other into new shapes, how one underlined the other, drew the other, outlined the other, how that was always changing. She thought of their life together, how after five years they were learning to put their mark on each other, let themselves be shaped a bit by the other. They knew what it felt like inside to be the other, to use the other's muscles, and they knew how the air felt on the other's skin. Each defined themself and also the other. The dividing line was flexible, always different. They gave their bodies to each other and gave back what they received. One body, a divided body, two bodies, one body, both body. She wrote down some words.

She heard him come across the yard and up on to the veranda. She heard him start to fill the tub with jugs of water, at first a tinkling splash then a deeper one. She wiped her sweaty hands on her red and yellow kimono. She called to him that she was going to come out and share his bath, was that all right, and he shouted back yes, bring a bottle of wine and a couple of glasses.

6

On Writing

ON WRITING A NOVEL

Commissioned for the Summer Masterclass series and published in the *Times Higher Educational Supplement*, 15 August 1995

Since proverbs are seen as one of the most clichéd forms of folk wisdom it is possible to utter, I hereby offer you a list of my favourites, straight from the horse's mouth, in order to warn you to take everything I say with a large pinch of salt.

In for a penny, in for a pound. Don't start to write a novel just because you think it might be a nice thing to do, or because you think you ought to, in order to demonstrate your creativity. Just because we all use language every day for talking and for telling stories, it doesn't follow that we've all got to write novels. Some of us turn out to have a flair for gardening or mud-wrestling. Only the energy of desire, passionate and obsessive, will steer you through the difficulties involved and sustain you through the months and probably years of hard work required. Don't write a novel in order to get rich quick; you'd do better going into the City. Most novelists are poor and have second jobs. Don't write a novel in order to become famous; this cannot be guaranteed. Don't write a novel for cynical reasons; you will write badly. Write a novel only if you know there's no alternative.

You must love language, your demanding medium. You must love playing with it, attending to it, endlessly reworking it, learning from it what can and can't be done with it. Language isn't just a transparent pane of glass through which we view the real world.

It is part of the real world. It is matter. Shaping it affects how we see things. Think of liquid glass, blown glass, stained glass. Think of a window-pane that is dusty or cracked or absent. Words are your stuff, as material as paint or clay, to be put together in patterns and shapes (otherwise known as novels) that may end up figurative or abstract or somewhere in between.

A stitch in time saves nine. In your daily life you are probably required to bestow kindness, sympathy and sensitive attention on others. Start now to direct these helpful energies towards yourself. You will need them later on when you get stuck or depressed or feel it's not worth keeping going. Start now to cultivate the writer's virtues of unsociability, love of solitude and silence, selfishness, and aggression. Selfishness allows you to do what you want: write a novel; rather than care for others most of the time. Aggression allows you to be destructive: of old literary forms; of your own clichés; towards language itself. You break up old word-patterns then reshape them into new ones. Be childishly cruel and curious, picking the wings off a word-fly in order to see how it's made. Childishness has no shame in recognising and valuing a subject tabooed by the grown-ups. You can go back to being a nice person when you are not writing. Also, start now to record your dreams, as a stock of images and new ways of seeing, and as a source for recognising the wilder excesses of, say, lust and rage within yourself. This will enable you, later on, to tap deep psychic energies for writing, to create realistic characters (if that's what you want to do), and to find the necessary vibrant forms of expression.

Don't run before you can walk. Do just a little bit every day. Don't be dismayed at how bad it is. Rewrite it next day. And again next day. You might have half an hour for writing each day. Write exactly fifty words: a good exercise in honing and pruning, in realising how you can juggle with words to make them fit, how they go on being plastic and malleable as you play with them.

Steadily, your little bits will mount up. At the end of a year, see what you've got. Going step by step you realise a novel is an integration of bits and pieces. You don't have to map it all out in advance, unless you're writing a tightly plotted thriller, and even then it's fun to surprise yourself. Don't feel you have to be totally in control. Advance bravely into the unknown, step by step. I always start with a visual image which is currently obsessing me, which might translate into a question. Exploring this image, trying to answer this question, is the route of the novel.

You can't make a silk purse out of a sow's ear. Perhaps you don't want to. Perhaps a hide wallet is what you're after. But in any case, form is everything. The demands of the subject help you invent a form. Stretch yourself, to find out what you really want to write about. Then create a form that expresses that, so that the form and the subject become part of each other, inseparable. I was recently writing about a woman who was neurotically obsessed with making lists. The literary form I used, therefore, to express her in action, was the list. I discovered that her lists functioned as her diary, and that what she left out, or lied about, was as interesting as her attempts to tell the truth. So let yourself experiment with lots of the forms into which written language composes itself. Don't assume that you have automatically got to write in the past tense, in the third person, using a more or less omniscient narrator. See what suits your subject best.

You mustn't put new wine in old bottles. The new wine of hot or cool modern/postmodern consciousness sometimes, paradoxically, enjoys maturing in the old bottles of folk tale or fairy tale, for example. My problem with conventional realism and naturalism is that, by surveying (usually from above, in the manner of that old-fashioned author God on his cloud) the surface, this kind of single-voiced narration often leaves out the unconscious, the soul, all the deep feelings of the body. A chaotic, plural narrative coming from the inside, the underneath, the edge, may be more telling and powerful. It all depends on what you want to do: follow convention or bend it. We all, I think, write out of our own wishes and fears, our own fantasies of desire or anxiety; the pressure of these, once recognised, will help you hear a voice, get to know a character, find a form. People often say: oh you mustn't write about yourself. But you can write about the things you haven't done yet but want to. You can write from a part of yourself you disapprove of. I can write about nasty ladies because they exist inside me, bitchy and murderous. You can get lots of comedy this way, not just horror. It's good to break your own rules once they start feeling oppressive. I've had a thing for ten years about how I *must not* write omniscient narration, so I am currently writing one, because it's the story of a woman who wants to control others, to straitjacket them in her stories. Similarly, having listened to the critics tell me for twenty years that confessional writing, especially by feminists, is a Bad Thing, I have finally plucked up courage to let my feminist nasty lady walk into a confessional and start confessing to the person on the other side of the grille: who may be a priest or you or my aunt.

All that glisters is not gold. Be ruthless about rewriting and redrafting until each sentence, each paragraph, and so each chapter, and finally the whole thing, is as good as you can possibly make it. As the novel progresses and changes you will find that you need to rewrite, anyway, as you discover your focus, your tone, what kind of narrative you need to write. I think it's a sign of strength and commitment to be prepared to redraft. Why should you have to get it right first time? If a first draft comes out badly and glibly, with great ease, you often feel complete despair at your worthlessness as a writer; then you simply have to set to and find ways to slow yourself down. Pretending to be a camera helps. You can jump-cut scene to scene, slow your speed, change focus. You can take a scene twenty times if you need to. You might decide to include several of these in the end, not just one. When you have performed your alchemy, and got your gold, and included glister too if that's what you need, then, and only then, are you ready to approach an agent and/or a publisher. Most unknown writers are judged by their first paragraph or first page, so this needs to be as well written as you can possibly make it. Don't be afraid if this takes a long time. You learn the craft as you go. You improve with practice. Somebody once said: genius is eternal patience. Well, we can all strive towards that. Your first novel may be fresh, original and passionate. It won't, perhaps, be your best. That's all right. You don't have to be an overnight success, a child prodigy. Take your time.

A friend in need in a friend indeed. Writing is a solitary business, and from time to time it's good to have someone to talk about it with. Ours is not a public, café culture, in the main, so you have to organise to meet other writers, whether this means supper with a friend or finding the right sort of local group. The Brontës had each other, but nearest and dearest aren't always able to give you the critical support you need. They may not like you writing. They may not like the new, assertive, selfish you. Whereas other writers, the right ones, may help you spot your strengths and build on them. A good course can help in this respect, especially for beginners. It can help to find a peer group even if you want to be an eternal outsider. Writer friends can help you deal with writer's block and see it as normal, the usual start to the writer's day. They can swap gossip and advice about publishing. In an ideal world, the publishing editor who takes on your novel will be brave and caring enough to comment on your text, and will respect your decisions about redrafting it yet again. *Bon courage.*

WRITING *DAUGHTERS OF THE HOUSE*

Observer, 13 October 1992

Only quite recently I realised that all my novels so far have dealt with homeless women, women who in some way are disqualified or don't belong. This sixth book alters that pattern, deals with inheritance: of a house, and of its secrets.

Various themes, images and questions sloshed around in my imagination, mad cocktail. I wrote the novel to try and answer the questions, explore the images and themes, and experiment anew with just what the novel as a form can do.

The core image was visual. I was haunted, obsessed, by the picture of a red virgin appearing to a little girl in the woods. I tracked this back to my own childish desire, aged nine or so, ardently Catholic, to have a vision of Our Lady, like St Bernadette. I knew it was impossible: you had to live in the countryside in the south of France, not in an English suburb. But it was fun, aged forty, to give myself permission to explore that desire, to realise it. All to do with mothers, real and ideal, of course.

Simultaneously I was haunted by news stories in the papers about the resurgence of Fascism in Europe, the desecration of graves in Jewish cemeteries in France, the red swastikas daubed on the headstones. An article in the French paper *Libération* about this time suggested that Fascism was the ghoul, the undead, the return of the repressed; this gripped and focused my imagination.

I began to think about my parents' history during the war, and that of the French side of my family who had endured the Nazi occupation in Normandy. Chucked out of their house. I began to wonder about how history was recorded. Could little girls be responsible historians or were they inevitably unreliable narrators? The feminine view is often dismissed as narrow. I liked the idea of exploiting that, of using a feminine peep-hole and perspective, of letting something apparently little (girls' perceptions) stand for, swivel towards, something big (the suffering of France in the war). At the same time I was dealing with two characters who didn't want to be partial and restricted at all; both Léonie and Thérèse, my two protagonists, wanted to be omniscient narrators of their own stories, and soon engaged in tough quarrelling. This gave me my form, at last. Thérèse, the holy prig, was trying to write a spiritual autobiography to justify herself. Simultaneously, Léonie, the houseproud lover of material possessions, was drawing up an inventory of the contents of the house. The novel, I realised, had to embody both narratives, give them both room. At last I could get going and start writing. All this thinking and chaos and muddle was at last getting me somewhere. After a year of false starts, waiting, thinking, reading, doodling, I was off.

One of the things I did was return to the saint who'd fascinated and disgusted me as a child: Thérèse of Lisieux, the Little Flower, the would-be priest and martyr who'd settled for the crazy heroism of life as an enclosed Carmelite, at the end of the nineteenth century, and whose autobiography, a text piling hysteria upon mysticism, would have fascinated Freud. I used Thérèse's account as a springboard for trying to imagine what a modern female saint might be like.

My narrative tried to weave all these odd bits together. My love of thrillers was a challenge: could I write something with a whodunnit plot that included elements of the Gothic? The haunted house, the *unheimlich* home, the taboo maternal body; these connected to my theme of safe places, refuges from Nazi terror.

The writing took about a year, working seven days a week whenever possible. For the first time in my writing life, I set myself a target of a thousand words a day: I'd just given up smoking and wanted to make sure I produced something. It was a joy to discover that rather than worry about cigarettes, rather than have a smokescreen between me and words, there was just me concentrating on language. I hurled myself at it. Sometimes I drifted off, just stared at the curtains. I ate well, delicious lunches in one hand while I typed with the other then scribbled on the draft in pen and ink then rewrote it, several times. Writer's block was a regular companion I learned to greet like a dancing partner; silence alternated with bursts of forging forwards.

Dreams showed me the way through. I was stuck over the ending until I dreamed what it was. I dreamed I was the daughter of the house, going down into the cellar and starting to dig. Under the heap of sand there I discovered the end of the novel. Then I could go back over it and pull it all together. It ended with a woman finding words; a nod towards the imperative of the next novel.

POST-SCRIPT

A rewritten version of the afterword in
The Semi-Transparent Envelope by Nicole Ward Jouve,
Susan Sellers and Sue Roe (Marion Boyars, 1994)

> *Life is not a series of gig lamps symmetrically arranged, but a luminous halo, a semi-transparent envelope surrounding us from the beginning of consciousness to the end.*
>
> Virginia Woolf

The semi-transparent envelope: it's hard to see the writing inside; a bill? torn-up fragments of letters? When you write a novel you have to make out the form. Discover it. Find it. (Latin *invenio*: I find, I come upon, and so I invent.) You find the form by meditating on the demands of the subject matter.

Inspiration: something arrives, swims up, a message in a bottle bobs tantalisingly and you peer at it, not quite able to make it out. That pearly paper of the window in the envelope; that rippled glass of the floating bottle. You have to destroy something, paper or glass, to get at what's inside. Lovely aggressive destruction, like when I was a child making mud dishes and smashing the porcelain head of an antique doll.

I begin with a haunting, an obsession. Something's nagging at me, bothering me. A visual image appears, or a bit of one. I translate it into words. A dead nun in the school chapel: from this, like silk spun from a cocoon, eventually came the whole of my first novel. I write novels to understand the wordless images, spin a story around them that will lay them, like ghosts. Also to answer questions: can mothers truly love daughters? Does a woman belong in this world and is she allowed to have a house of her own?

At the same time I write novels to explore the form, to find out just what it can do. Different each time. The content (those images, those nagging questions) shapes the form; only that form can demonstrate that content. Yes, form *is* content. The story of a woman obsessed with material possessions *had* to be told as her inventory of the contents of her house; the story of the cousin she quarrelled with *had* to be a saint's autobiography that could quarrel with the version contained in the inventory. Clash of points of view; clash of forms. I want to write in a way that relishes language, its materiality like paint. The language is what matters. It has, is, body.

I might spend from six months to a year, these days, struggling to discover the form the novel could take, before I discover it. *Struggle* can mean just sitting quietly attending to all the problems, naming them, listening to them. Jim, who's a painter, always says to me: make the problem part of the subject. You do that at the level of content, also of form. So during this period, when the imagination needs to be fed and stimulated, I read voraciously (literary theory when it comes under my nose, thrillers, Edwardian guidebooks filched from my aunt's house, books which arrive randomly as gifts or cast-offs), I record my dreams (the novel always starts here), I scribble madly in chaotic notebooks, I make lots of false starts, I make notes, I doodle.

There's nothing I like better than this hermit's life of writing, solitude all day and every day, seven days a week if I so choose, when I've got the money to write full time, that is. It depends – on sales and royalties, on unpaid bills. Even when the writing is going badly or not at all (silence and writer's block are normal, inextricably part of the writing process, you learn to trust in absence and inability and powerlessness and the need to wait quietly and patiently), this is where I want to be: in my study, on my own, all day long. (At night, when the working day is done, I want all the pleasures of conviviality; conversation and wine and food and sex.) Until I was twenty or so I thought I had a religious vocation, wanted to become a Carmelite, spend my life in prayer, in silence. It strikes me, looking at what I've written here, that writing is a bit like waiting on God (also like Keats's negative capability): trusting in the darkness, opening yourself up to what comes, being empty. *Making* actually feels very active to me. Perhaps prayer can be too. I think I've invented my own version of the convent, becoming a writer: no Mother Superior needed; lots of good food as muse (see below); an image of God changing from a distant, absent, invisible and frightening authority figure of either sex (sometimes – I mean I have many images of God) to that of a close, warm, present and nourishing body, which first I've imaged as female and maternal but now also find in the body of the man I love and desire. Writing's a bisexual practice: you have to be both active and passive; 'masculine' and 'feminine' need to be in relation; mother relates to child inside the self; all this is an ever-changing dance, never static. I don't use the word 'androgynous' for this – to me it implies fixedness, transcendence. I prefer 'bisexual'.

I want to put in a word on food and its relationship to writing, because it matters to me. Writing is a physical act. I don't use a word processor (I *always* want to call it a food processor) but a tiny ancient portable typewriter with very bouncy keys you can hit satisfyingly hard, and with smudgy ink ribbons. I like scribbling in pen over typed drafts; I like the act of the hand moving, the traces of ink, the sound of the nib scritch scritch scritch; the palimpsests I produce, memory encoded on the page; the history of three drafts, perhaps, visible on a single sheet. That's all very physical, close to drawing (I wanted to be a painter as well as a nun, was devastated when I failed art O Level with grade Z). Writing feels like pulling something out of my insides; I've made it inside, now must draw it out, put it out. It's painful or pleasurable, depending on how the work's going, but it diminishes and empties me, I've lost part of myself, I become hungry. Meals are fuel and reward. I also find that cooking myself a quick but delicious lunch, to be eaten at the typewriter, will get me through my writer's block of the morning and produce pages of writing. I eat with one hand and type with the other. The mother in me feeds the baby in me.

Mother and baby co-operate to produce the writing. The baby is the artist but is helped by the mother. On the other hand, too much food at midday can act as a tranquilliser and send me to sleep. Sometimes I unconsciously wish for this, as a way of escaping the stress, resistances and anxieties of writing, and hanker for a fix of olive oil on my lunch, a dose of sleepiness and work-avoidance. It would be more glamorous, obviously, to be hooked on whisky . . .

So there's cooking and eating, and there's taking little naps like semicolons to divide the day (or long siestas when I need to escape for longer), and then there's housekeeping. Writing, for me, is a way of keeping house; building myself the house I felt I wasn't allowed to have when I was younger. Now that I've actually got the longed-for little house of my own in France, which is where I live when I'm writing, I find that housework is quite enjoyable. It acts as a helpful image of rootling about in my imagination and re-ordering it, sorting things out, choosing what to keep and what to throw out. Words, pictures, dust, images. Though I spend more time trying to polish sentences than I do polishing the table and chairs.

MAKING IT UP: ON WRITING *FLESH AND BLOOD*

New Writing 4: an anthology edited by A. S. Byatt and Alan Hollinghurst (Vintage, 1995)

Notebook dated 1 December 1991

I'm starting to speed up now. Here we go. Towards a new novel. The beginning of one, just beginning to be marked on my windscreen.

Write the novel according to some surrealist game – use randomness, the unconscious, very deliberately, in its construction? Make this clear in the text? I don't know yet.

paper with the graininess of porridge, or polenta, or purée of chick peas

a woman's desire for passion freely expressed, for personal freedom power autonomy – at the beginning she thinks that to have this she'll need power over others? So she founds her convent? The Order of the Dark Star

a light in the darkness
illumination; radiance
the burning bush
light in the trees; in the grass
light held by darkness and enclosed by it, irradiating it
arise, shine, for thy night hath come

n.b. fifteenth-century narrative paintings of saints' lives

all the living and the dead can be in it, and all the present and the past

she'll found her new religion out of rebellion against the mother, very much, as well as against the father. Rage and resistance. She'll play a ritualised battle of the Mothers against the Daughters – tournament joust.

Her mother closed her eye against her, refused to see or acknowledge her reality, and her father opened his eye of sex upon her and pronounced her *his.* So her only identity was as her father's fantasy sex object. Nothing from her mother to fall back on. She needed her mother to stand by her during her Oedipal crisis but her mother couldn't. She feared she'd damaged and done away with her mother. So part of the myth of her new religion will re-enact this family drama and attempt to resolve it. All she knows is power relationships. She seeks to dominate others in her turn. She's frightened of power yet longs for it. She's full of sadistic fantasies. So have the mother damaged in some way – and a miraculous cure.

to write a maternal narrative – that lets a mother speak, that creates a text about pain and grotesque comedy and confusion, that can face all this, that can contain it – so that text somehow enacts motherhood. Form and content are mother–daughter. The text expresses that. The surrealism in the novel will come from details being heightened from the ordinary and the mundane just a little into the bizarre – so you'll still see the connection to the everyday

Write the novel as a series of contrasts between family history, the 'real', and the mystical mythology? Which is the mythologising of the former? Write the novel in layers, it'll have to be layers, can't just be one narrative, layers of mother and father on top of the child like a *mille-feuille.*

dream: a silver angel flying very fast across the heavens at night with her hands clasped

sort of cannibalistic eucharistic ritual – the eating of the body of the mother – and then her magical regeneration, restoration

a central mystery in which people change, are metamorphosed, into the opposite sex? and one woman becomes two and then back to one again?

the narrative voice *enacts* this metamorphosis, *is* polymorphously perverse

a religion about the meaning of birth and death, food central to express it, food growing in the ground; the garden of memory

Usually I write about the unconscious erupting into reality, using a sort of psychoanalytical model. This time write about the unconscious *as* reality, with 'reality' breaking in occasionally. Hence, I now see, my current interest in surrealism

We took Beewee to Etretat, sea like blue milk, warm as summer, the grey pebbles, later as the sun began to sink the stones on the beach glistened blue, the cliffside went golden, we lay and looked at the smooth water, the waves draw in and out, hiss and drag over the shingle nutcracker death has got Beewee in his curved claws

Notebook dated 13 March 1992

Somehow connected to my idea of maternal narrative: one aspect of this novel's text is to be something written by a mother for her daughter – to delight and instruct her; a gift; a pattern book; a courtesy book; inventing a world fit for a daughter to live in. Jokes too. Also erotic and bawdy. And then – the idea of a sex-change as part of the narrative/technique, part of the subject of metamorphosis, part of the plot. Put side by side different people, different pieces of story and storytelling, play with that, let the reader work out the trick, the illusion, that what looks like a simple sequence may not be. Patch it in.

layer after layer to go through: sheets of paper, clothes, skins; so make the stories themselves do the metamorphosing, one into another, one enclosing another; all to do with change; so the reader has to experience something bisexual – both penetration (into the heart of the book, its hidden centre) and enclosing, being enclosed (cf. Sidney's *Arcadia*)

one story will be someone who is one sex in England and another in France, set in Etretat on the shore, fishing life, the Impressionists coming to paint; also an eighteenth-century story about reason versus emotion, vice versus virtue, with the Marquis de Sade in it each story is the mother of the next one/the deceitful narratives of the turncoats!

it's on the level of image, of symbol, that she heals herself and finds her mother again; and that's where it happens – in the dark room, at first she thinks it's empty but then—

sudden scary surrealistic change is the stuff of childhood – that's the experience

I'm scared of writing about religion, of being mocked, of sounding twee, and I'm scared of all the letting go involved, the plunge into chaos, not-knowing, wildness, loss of self, in order to write

Dacia was saying today, quoting Barthes, that writing is playing with the body of the mother – well, is that why I feel so blocked, because I feel not allowed to play that play? She was suggesting daughters too, not just Barthes the son, could play with the mother's body. I'm not so sure! but it was a very powerful, very sweet, evocation she made. I'm writing about the consequences of the absent mother: grotesque women; oppressed women are not necessarily *nice*. n.b. I suddenly realised why I am reading De Sade – my desire to write about feminine masochism – though so far his female characters appear to be solely emblematic, representatives of Virtue and Morality opposed to Man. Boring.

Notebook dated 3 July 1992

We drove to Etretat early morning, no cars or people, utterly empty, grey-blue and sparkling, sun on rain. Then returned via Vattetot and Bénouville, tiny coves and hamlets, mad Edwardian summerhouses sprouting turrets and balconies. Now in Domfront on its high hill. We nearly bought a presbytery, seventeenth-century with gun emplacements, a *potager*, holy pics, huge cellar full of cider. Sunset like a bloom on fruit. Milky golden light and the crackle of sun. People working with pitchforks on the verges, raking cut hay. We looked and looked. Also of course you see modern France, its bureaucracies and agrobusiness, etc; tho on this journey I encountered no racism; yeah I speak as a sloppy sentimental lover of my homeland I expect; but the peace and quiet, well. Something to cherish. Back in London's grime and traffic jams and noise oh I hated it, I wanted to go back to France. OK I love Soho, I even love the Holloway Road because of the people I meet in the shops, but I hate the noise booming around, the dog turds, the aggressive mad driving.

the form of the novel will make it appear it goes in in in – but in fact the worlds revealed could just as well seem to be external ones; what is 'inside' and what is 'outside'? n.b. try to go right beyond Catholic imagery this time, right through it and out the other side

RIP Beewee died 28 October at 5 a.m.

finally the spirit left the house, that noisy angry one, she upped & went in the middle of the night, my fear evaporated when something else – a warm close maternal voice – took over and calmed me down. I felt I'd re-connected with all the childhood waking terrors I'd ever had in that house at night – and I was a small child again, and then at last consoled, a warm presence was near to me. I fell asleep at last.

Walk through a hidden valley to the sea, empty secret beach we discovered, fell down on to it, like being born Jim said. It was Le Tilleul – which I knew as a child.

Notebook dated 1 January 1993

a corpse arriving in a sledge drawn quickly across the packed snow, the girl hears the sledge arrive at night, it whistles in over the snow

remember the huge rainbow that arched over the house at Criquetot after Beewee's funeral, remember the wild violets in the woods and the anemones and the primroses, the coarse salt we scattered under our feet to melt the black ice, those two deer we saw fleeing across the track in the Bois des Loges, and how at the end the house smelled of chocolate and yeast

the pattern of the novel: each bit told by a different character; are they all linked; collecting up all the bits, joining them up

loss: try to find that lost place again; paradise regained; this is the novel tugging ahead wanting to get written; supposing the novel's shape were a spiral?

Female narrators in the first half and then male? The female ones can't really see themselves, their shadow; and the male ones see women in a particular way.

Hard to make something out of nothing, haul it out, form it. I feel tired all the time, I want to escape, into sleep. Difficult narratives, writing in the third person because for some reason I feel I must for these parts of it. When you're using the first person and become possessed by a voice then it can really flow. Chaos and muddle and confusion and despair and difficulty. I don't know what I'm doing. I'm writing badly and superficially. Terrible thick lethargy. I'm not giving myself to writing with love and abandon, I lack love and commitment. You have to give yourself to the writing for the sheer love of it, there is no other way to do it, that's what it demands. I fear that, because it brings up the pain rage terror of childhood, writing makes me re-experience that, too painful. I couldn't just leave the pain and terror at Criquetot, by deciding not to buy the house, because it's inside me.

What am I frightened of? That I shall die. That I'll jump in, give myself totally, and there'll be nothing and no one there and so I'll die. Do all writers have this terror? I don't know. I don't know anyone to discuss it with. It's only novels that tap these deep-seated feelings of insecurity, this terror; never poems. Is it masochistic to keep plunging back into it? Can I learn somehow that writing, diving into language, is not the same as being a terrified angry child? Could I learn to give myself to language, to writing, without these fears and terrors? I thought I'd dealt with them and yet again they resurface. In *Daughters of the House* I wrote about material things, in Léonie's inventory, I anchored myself that way. Things I could *touch.* It got me over the worst. Beewee's death ended my repression, my childhood in that house – I no longer had to be just the good niece, the good loving girl, I could begin to accept how *angry* my child-self was.

Notebook dated 18 May 1993

trying to use something slippery and unfixed as words, where the signifiers are arbitrary, invented, to express something I feel is *true* – to find some deep truth – the truth of the lives of our bodies in this world – to express it – the words themselves feel sacred and true to me, not arbitrary at all. I've got a religious attitude to language and I always have had. Religion's in the unconscious and erupts up from there.

Chaos and uncertainty – that's what I'm living in. Hold it, contain it. Didn't Mr Keats have something to say about this? Stick with it dear.

How would I like to live? It's not a question I've felt able really to ask myself before when I was homeless, with little money. Free in a certain way, very unfree in others. Now I've *got* to think about it, because the choices are opening up. I've also *got* to think about what I really want to write about in order to get going again on the novel which got stuck while I was feeling a bit taken over by others, that I was writing for them now, not for myself any more.

Now I've bought La Poivière I want to go and live in it for ever and work in the garden, that's what I want to do

Notebook dated October 1993

When I'm here at La Poivière, sitting on the front step looking at the view of fields and hills or stacking wood or slashing brambles or staring into the fire or painting the walls or just pottering about, I'm in a state of happiness – ordinary – this is my spot on the planet, I belong, I am meant to be here. That bliss of childhood: being free out of doors, being out of the house, not needing to think about myself, being able to let go and just be part of the landscape, a happiness born in the body like the warmth of the earth, the earth's warm breath.

My fears and doubts about writing when I'm doing it – because of those childhood feelings of: what I feel is not valid and must not be spoken. Repression. Prohibition. Don't forget this. So it's not just fear of going mad when the self dissolves in order to create; it's also fear of what's inside me coming out, that it's bad because critics (e.g. Grandpère the old patriarch) said so in childhood. Don't forget this.

Days spent alone here writing. The house to myself all day long completely empty and completely silent. I sat in the sitting room so that I could have sunlight to write and see the birds on the bird-table, and the novel just rushed out like a river underground spouting out, pages and pages every day. Very convent-like, that was the image I kept getting; long hours of silence and work. I invented a new sort of gnocchi. I cook much better out here because I'm so happy, I've got a light touch, it comes right. Now that feels true for the writing too. I've never ever felt such pleasure in writing as I do here. Partly I know because I've reached the magic halfway point from which you survey the end, unwritten yet, but you know you're on the way, yes it's like knowing an orgasm is building and you will come, but I do think it is being able to live here in this house that makes all the difference. A home of my own, a place to live I can't be thrown out of. Now I feel I belong to the human race. Planting my French root back into France, finishing my novel.

ON SELF-CENSORSHIP

Brangle magazine, Queens University, Belfast, Spring 1997

Self-censorship is difficult to write about because to function well it functions unconsciously: if I'm affected by it I probably don't know it. I associate it with writer's block. When I'm stuck and can't write, I end up discovering self-censorship is at work. My last novel, *Impossible Saints*, was very hard to get off the ground because it drew on my adolescent sexual feelings for my father. In a Catholic family these had to be repressed. They made me feel wicked. The taboo on incest meant I could not recognise desires it took many years to discover were normal. The Catholic Church, with its disgusting stress on shame and guilt, taught me to shut up, or tried to. At the same time it made me into a writer: words would insist on bursting up and out, words about women and our buried unconscious lives.

All writing is of course a struggle out of silence to find the right words, or the best you can do.

Nowadays I link self-censorship with narrative perspective. Although I continue to be inspired by my childhood and by my unconscious, I translate the stuff more and more. Art feels more true to me than reportage, because it's made of metaphors, layers of meanings not just one simple truth. For example, last year I had a series of painful encounters with my stepson which made me feel very hurt and angry. The enormous temptation was to put him into a story, get my own back, make myself look saintly and good, by writing omnisciently in the third person about him and me, with him as the villain. I'm not ashamed of my rage and hurt and wishes for revenge but *perhaps* they were better expressed to him (we finally sorted it out, kissed and made up), and *perhaps* that fantasised story would have read as a whinge of a superego-ridden victim: look how sensitive and sweet I am, how nasty he is, love me please love me. This is a plea by a child to an authority. I had enough of that in my youth, going to confession and having to plead for absolution. It's a discourse, finally, of masochism. More interesting to me is the solution I have found: to let those powerful feelings and desires fuel a translation, find what Eliot called the objective correlative in the 'outer' world, rewrite 'Cinderella' perhaps, sympathetically, from the stepmother's point of view, concentrate less on what I think happened (reportage by the conscious mind driven by the superego or punitive conscience) than on what I fear might have happened or what I wanted to happen. I'm released from guilt about exposing my stepson because I'm writing about what didn't happen: my fears or wishes about what *might* have happened, and also my imagination can take flight, writing about it, the unconscious bit, the id, which is wilder and sexier and angrier and more interesting (to me, very often) than the conscious mind which wants to write naturalism or realism and stress This Really Happened. So you can see I've evolved an aesthetic technique for jumping over moral problems. Should I write about those I love given that they can't answer back? No. I don't want to hurt those I love (I did it enough when I was young after all, when I so needed to shout about the power of mothers for good and evil, in my first two novels, and my mother, I'm glad to say, six books on, is really talking to me now and has been heard to say I've improved) *but* I can translate the feelings into stories, let the feelings take me into the unknown. Discover something new. Far more fun than writing about what I think I already know.

Where does self-censorship overlap with political correctness and do we need more precise and subtle terms for trying to respect how other people feel? I can't write in the first person as a black character. It would feel to me imperialistic and intrusive to do so. It feels far more necessary to excavate the racism of white people and write about that. More and more I've been thinking about that. It's a question of narrative perspective again; it all depends on how you do it. I can't write omnisciently in the third person about black people either. I suffered all my life from men's fantasies about women masquerading as the truth; I can't do that in my turn. Yet I don't want to be silenced. My socialist and feminist politics make me reach out in solidarity to others while acknowledging difference, my privileged history. So far I'm concentrating on tackling my own 'whiteness'. That doesn't feel like self-censorship or soppy liberalism to me, but other people might see it that way. I do believe that I'm free to write about whatever I want to. Desire lights up the subject and suggests a perspective on it. I don't believe in characters in the traditional realistic sense, but if I hear a black person's voice start talking in my imagination then I shall certainly want to set down what it says. At this point, I can hear one or two writer friends roaring with laughter and saying: just get on with it.